EATING CHOCOLATE & WATCHING THE MOON

READERS RESPOND

"Catherine Steinberg is a real feminine powerhouse of knowledge. The first time we met I was taken with her inner strength, passion, and willingness to show up for the hard issues. I was introduced to Catherine as Rubybear, and I am delighted she wrote a memoir for her story. Through periods of difficult loss, Rubybear learned to trust her intuition as "medicine." It is this powerful medicine that she generously shares with all of us. Readers will be gifted with the understanding of how to work with their intuition and nature for guidance. They will learn about shamanism, the role of the divine feminine and expressive therapies as ways to find meaning, love, and transformation in their lives. This book is a treasure and Catherine Steinberg is a brilliant writer who will help you move through your losses and find your greatest opportunities."

— Sandra Ingerman, MA international shamanic teacher and award winning author of 13 books including *Soul Retrieval* and *Walking in Light*

"Steinberg's memoir illuminates the pathos and ecstasy of being bound to a strong yet vulnerable physical body and simultaneously always-beyond it, evolving, and yet unchanging. Because she holds her journey's many paradoxes in suspension, never claiming to know, only to see, she uncovers wisdom at every turn of her fate, and for us, her readers, her story is a deep-resonating absolute gift: richly textured, tenderhearted, unforgettable."

— Gray Jacobik, Ph.D., Professor Emerita, Poet & Painter

"I loved this book. The medicine and divine connection that comes from communing with nature, the complexity and karmic web of our relationships and reunions, the quest for meaning pushing us deeper into our spiritual path and intuition, and of course the beauty and life lessons from motherhood... these themes resonated with me deeply."

— Lauren Dailey, RYT and Ayurvedic Educator

CATHERINE N. STEINBERG

Eating Chocolate & Watching the Moon

*Spiritual Awakening
through Loss
and Karmic Resolution*

RUBYBEAR CREATIONS
Guilford, Connecticut
2024

"I No Longer Pray," Chelan Harkin from *Susceptible to Light*. Used by permission. www.chelanharkin.com

"For Those Who Have Far to Travel" © Jan Richardson from *Circle of Grace: A Book of Blessings for the Seasons*. Used by permission. janrichardson.com

Cover painting by Catherine N. Steinberg
Book Design by Words by Jen (Branford, CT)
Printed in the U.S.A.

Memoir
Inspiration & Personal Growth
Spirituality

ISBN: 979-8-218-45210-0

) ● (

DEDICATION

This book is dedicated to all my karmic allies, visible and invisible, but especially to my husband, Marvin, and our son, Aaron Taos.

If not for them, this journey never would have taken place.

Throughout time may we be joined in Love and Light.

CONTENTS

FOREWORD

Most memoirs about the theme of overcoming the odds focus upon a single issue; it might be a health crisis, some kind of deficiency, or the loss of a loved one. We rarely find one book that contains multiple challenges, like Catherine's does, yet her triumphs are universally relevant. The odds she overcame were not just physical and intellectual, but also spiritual and emotional. And it's the ways these are intertwined in her story that I found so fascinating. As you will see, she shares some unusual approaches for readers dealing with layers of losses, serious setbacks or tragedies.

When I first met Catherine Nogas Steinberg, a licensed marriage and family therapist, she was teaching a shamanic painting course in Madison, Connecticut. Her multifaceted competencies impressed me from the start. Therapist. Teacher. Artist. Shaman. And those were just the ones visible at first glance.

That meeting was nearly a decade ago. Back then I was struggling to write a memoir of my own. Her class offered an alternative method for accessing deeper realms, and I had some blockages to overcome. After reading her bio and course description online, I signed up.

As a former CBS News journalist, and global management development pioneer myself, I'd lived in the factual, evidenced-based domain. Traveling the world, I'd been paid to write about it, and other people, not myself. It was far more difficult to sit still and deeply excavate my own psyche. Yet what drew me to Catherine's class was our shared beliefs in the powers of intuition, art and expressive therapies.

Neither of us imagined at the start how the tables would turn over the years to come.

Her expertise helped me complete yet another draft of my first memoir and prepare for publication. My book, *The Importance of Paris*, won an IPPY (independent publishing award) in 2019. Afterwards many people asked me how I'd managed to do this, so I designed a workshop and invited them over to answer their questions. Thus began another career, teaching memoir writing.

Catherine attended my very first class, sitting around my dining room table, in rural Rhode Island. When it was her turn to read, she shared the scene about her past-life experiences, and I was hooked. Ever since, I've encouraged her to finish writing this book knowing others might benefit if they could read it. Eventually I became her content editor. Her manuscript grew more substantial and went through several drafts.

Now that her book is done, I marvel at the odds she's faced to finish it. In the time I've known Catherine, she's survived the pandemic, the death of her dear husband, and the loss of her best friend, Lianne S. Escher, whose book *A Mythic Sisterhood* is also a testament to female pluck.

Any one of these challenges might've derailed a would-be memoirist but Catherine persevered. After all, hers is a story about beating many odds, which included the heartbreaks of losing five pregnancies.

I won't reveal any spoilers here except to remind readers that Catherine could've coasted. A U.S. citizen, born white with some undeniable privileges, she might've never left suburbia. But she was brave and rebellious enough to resist the lure of social expectations, an early marriage and security after college. Instead she departed for some defining coming-of-age adventures, in South America, a place that turned out to be relevant to her past life.

Living and working abroad can be as challenging as dealing with deaths or divorces, but the expatriate life also builds character and resiliency. And Catherine had the gumption to stick with it for two years and reap some of the rewards. Facing culture shock, the adaptation cycle, acculturation and second-language trials were among the difficulties she encountered overseas. She also began questioning her North American upbringing, assumptions and prejudices. Those experiences broadened her sense of history and expanded her tolerance for ambiguity, all of which has stood her in good stead in the decades since, increasing her abilities to overcome the odds.

Suffice it to say, her adventures continued upon her return to the U.S. She made a cross-cultural marriage during the era when fewer than five percent of Americans did. And she dedicated her work life to helping others, as a therapist and shamanic practitioner. Even writing this book, to offer encouragement to others facing similar struggles, is a testament that will outlast her physical tenure.

I hope her story reaches the readers who need it most, especially the ones who have yet to learn about alternative approaches. Her practical results are undeniable despite employing so-called "woo woo" practices, which deserve more consideration by the modern medical establishment. Although she understands any outcomes will be unique to each individual, she opens the door for those who may never have imagined such approaches.

Eating Chocolate & Watching the Moon provides what it promises, "a spiritual awakening through loss and karmic resolution." Even to carry a healthy child to term, Catherine had to face new frontiers within herself as well as those in the outer world. What inspires me is how she discovered those internalized barriers and defied her inherited fears. By trusting her intuition, she became more self-directed. This empowered her to find the right remedies for her family.

Her story is good medicine. I salute those brave enough to read this book with an open mind and heart. May each of us dare to explore, do and share what we learn, as Catherine, Rubybear, has done.

— Cynthia F. Davidson —

)))
INTRODUCTION

The title of this book came long before I knew what its pages would say, or how the moon and chocolate might relate to my pregnancy losses and spiritual awakening. Like other firm nudges from my subconscious, I could recognize these words were important to remember and paid attention to this pair of phrases when they arrived. Both the moon and chocolate are deeply symbolic to many cultures, and to me personally. For a considerable number of years they also seemed to be beckoning, like mysterious clues, emanating from my psyche, inviting me to explore where they led. Did the moon and chocolate mean something particular to my healing story? And did their connection hold value for anyone else?

Those who've heard me tell parts of this story in person persuaded me to put it down in book form for a larger audience. They convinced me it might help those facing similar circumstances. I sincerely hope so. Back while I was grieving the loss of five pregnancies, I needed to hear a story like this. It has been my healing medicine.

Other moments in my life had already taught me to trust guidance bubbling up from my subconscious. And in my professional life as a psychotherapist, I'd seen my clients gain real results from following intuition after exhausting modern healthcare methods.

My spiritual awakening and its link to the moon and chocolate can be traced back to a night in 1996, when I was 45 years old and driving home to Connecticut from my spirituality group at the Women's Well of Interface in Boston. An almost full moon illuminated my way. At the time I was savoring a bar of fine chocolate. What a delight! Some of life's pleasures remain blessedly reliable.

An old memory came of a summer evening decades prior, when my mother had spied me, squatting in my red sandals, in a dark corner of our backyard.

"Cathy, what are you doing out there?" she cried.

My secret discovered, I replied in my three-year-old voice, "Eating chocolate and watching the moon."

Returning to that single scene is the summation of the divine for me. It symbolizes what deserves respect and full attention, and it represents the essence of sacredness: sweetness, sensuality, mystery, passion, play, earth, roots and sky, along with the felt connection to something far greater than oneself. Looking back, something else in that scene reconnects me to my life now: the mysteries of the moon's relationship to the sacred feminine, as revealed through the challenging difficulties on my journey to motherhood.

The moon often represents the feminine. It is said that women created the first calendars as they kept track of their bleeding times. With the lunar cycle mimicking our 28 day human menstrual cycle, our bodies also wax and wane consistently. The ancient matriarchal cultures worshiped moon goddesses. They celebrated the moon's powers of regeneration, the going in, the gestating and coming forth again. In my field of psychology, the Jungians cite the moon as the symbol of yin/feminine principles, plus the unconscious inner world of dreams and emotions. The mysteries of the sacred feminine, as represented by the moon, are still being revealed to me in this lifetime. Not done yet, my evolution continues. Now postmenopausal, I am embracing my inevitable cronehood and putting down my story in hopes it may someday benefit others and those not yet born.

And chocolate? Well, that relates tangibly to desire, longing and the tasting of life's sweetness! Chocolate often symbolizes life's joys. Yet the history of chocolate is far from joyful. Recent discoveries hint that humans have revered and traded cacao for many more centuries than previously realized. And the beans may have actually originated in the Amazon region of South America about 5,300 years ago.[1] The Mesoamerican Mayans and Aztecs considered cocoa a mystical gift of the gods. Believing it could activate a person's sacred energy, they also employed it as an aphrodisiac. Chocolate traveled along the commerce routes linking Central America and Mexico, and it was eventually usurped by the Spanish conquistadors. They shipped it back to Europe in the 16th century. There it became a treat for the royals who may have heard the rumors that Moctezuma II, the Aztec ruler, drank 50 cups a day.[2]

Many indigenous groups, including the Toltecs, made chocolate drinks for their religious ceremonies, initiations, and for marriages and the births of children. Sometimes it was mixed with blood for offerings to the gods. Chocolate was consumed mostly by the male members of the elite. The Spanish dubbed it *oro negro,* "black gold." Cacao seeds in Europe were prized primarily for medicinal purposes at first, although it became a common drink over time once sugar was added to it. Today, "cacao ceremonies" are held around the globe to use this drink as an elixir for emotional depth and personal revelation.[3]

As for the journey toward motherhood, I write for the women who believe one of the greatest joys in life is to have a child. By writing this book I hope to share what I learned during my long, somewhat unusual, quest to become a mother. My story is linked to the modern world's falling birthrates, increasing difficulties with conception, the rise of fertility clinics and adoptions too, for those who long to have children and a family life. My path to become a mother, and my particular challenges, may differ from others due to its specific spiritual context. This also linked me to my other lives in the lands where cacao comes from. And after awakening to those dimensions, I cannot separate motherhood from the sacred. Perhaps others who struggle to conceive and bear a child need to learn about this aspect. I wished I'd known about it sooner.

Trying to get pregnant and stay pregnant until full term catalyzed my spiritual growth. Facing pregnancy problems opened this dimension of my life in unexpected ways. Raised Roman Catholic, I'd left that way at age eighteen. In college, I studied various religions with the hope of finding a replacement, but none seemed to speak to me about what I most valued. Monotheistic organized religions are patriarchal, imaging god as a male. They cast women as less than, diminished and subservient to men. As a female I find these religions also tend to disrupt one's firsthand experience of the Divine. They insert their authorities, hierarchies, and stories in between our sacred knowing. I saw how these practices disempowered individuals, rather than encouraging us to have our own direct experiences, to establish our personal relationship with the Divine.

Yet I was always intrigued by the ineffable and unanswerable. The Nancy Drew mysteries I read as a child were replaced with Carlos Castenada and Lynn Andrews books as I became a young adult. But it wasn't until I started losing pregnancies that I became proactive in my search for meaning and guidance from the spiritual realm.

This book encompasses my learning experiences via dreams, past-life sessions, intuitive training and shamanic work, plus consultations with various spiritual teachers and psychics. It reveals how I came to share beliefs with Native American indigenous traditions and earlier priestess, pagan cultures. By journeying back to Nature Herself, I joined with others who have not lost their reverence for Her.

What is spirituality? I believe it is our third dimension, along with the body and the mind. In our busy, logic-minded Western world, we tend to neglect what is vital for gaining a sense of wholeness as a human being over our lifetimes. Ideally our spiritual practices cultivate that *felt* sense of connection to something greater than ourselves; whether you call it universal energy, nature or God. Although religions can be bridges to the spiritual, spirituality is larger than any single faith tradition, in my opinion. Spirit encompasses everything we hold sacred, that which deserves our attention and respect.

Often people with physical dis-ease or mental distress are also suffering from some form of spiritual neglect, as I have witnessed in my work as a psychotherapist as well as my own healing experiences. Those with chronic depression, anxiety and addiction disorders tend to recover more quickly when they engage with the spiritual dimension. Many studies prove this. All three areas of mind, body and spirit are equally important. We need to tend to them in proper proportion to live more balanced, healthy lives. Health in one area improves health in the others. Our bodies are needed to carry out our earthly purposes, and to house our minds and spirits. Our minds help us understand the world, each other and our emotions. We need to learn the stories and knowledge necessary to accomplish our spirit's intention in this incarnation, and to guide our mental and physical health in the physical realm. Our spirits give purpose and meaning to our lives, reminding us of our true soul essence via our emotional connections to love and joy and each other.

My motherhood journey also revealed karmic connections in our family. "Karma" is a Hindu and Buddhist concept. It is the belief in cause and effect, that your actions in one life, your good deeds and bad ones, will have an impact on your future lives. Karma is coupled with the belief in reincarnation taught by many religions. My husband and I had an opportunity in this lifetime to resolve issues from our past lives that did not end well, as readers will see. So in addition to being my story about becoming a mother, this book is an accounting of karmic completion, and the healing of unresolved woundings from a prior existence. I am convinced that this healing was key to my being able to become a mother in this lifetime after my husband and I had exhausted the offerings of the modern medical establishment.

I should mention my forty-plus years working as a marriage and family therapist. My interest in relationships, not just with significant others but with oneself, has been the major focus of my work life. From my first college psychology class, my fascination with the psyches or souls of individuals I work with has continued to grow. To understand my current clients and how they incorporate the physical, mental/emotional, social and spiritual dimensions of their lives helps them return to awareness and balance. And so my writing includes the psychological perspective because it is the great integrator of all our parts.

The motherhood journey, expanding the identity of the self and the completion of family karma within a spiritual context are the major themes of this book. Storytelling is the time-honored way for individuals to communicate their experiences with the vast depth of the sacred, and to show how Spirit works in our everyday lives. Many authors have written about spiritual issues from an intellectual perspective, providing conceptual frameworks that can be useful in understanding the spiritual dimension. But that is not my focus in this book. I believe we understand Spirit best from personally experiencing it, not merely reading about it. While I know some of my stories may seem far-fetched and unreal, others may be similar to my readers' own experiences. I only ask each reader to be open to the possibility of their realness for me. This may open you to the possibilities existing for you too.

I NO LONGER PRAY

I no longer pray—
now I drink dark chocolate
and let the moon sing to me.

I no longer pray—
I let my ancestors dance
through my hips
at the slightest provocation.

I no longer pray—
I go to the river
and howl my ancient pain
into the current.

I no longer pray—
I ache, I desire,
I say "yes" to my longing.

I no longer pray as I was taught
but as the stars crawl
onto my lap like soft animals at nighttime
and God tucks my hair behind my ears
with the gentle fingers of her wind
and a new intimacy is uncovered in everything,
perhaps it's that I'm finally learning
how to pray.

– Chelan Harkin, *Susceptible to Light*

CHAPTER 1
Shamanic Journey, March 12, 2018

My younger self is sitting with a handful of other children in a jungle clearing at the feet of the tribal teacher. The teacher seems to be Mayan and is speaking a language I do not know. He is instructing us by scratching symbols on a large rock with concentric circles that hold primal wisdom. I stand up and start twirling. Two Ravens transport me to a land with lush greenery and mountains. We stop to rest by a lake, which is called Atitlan in Guatemala. I am told that this is a place of refuge and beauty, free from "human stain." For me, it is Mother Earth.

As darkness sets in, the Ravens fly me over mountains and ice to the North Star, the place of our ancestors and those that have yet to be born. We are in an immense structure without ceiling or foundation. As I look around I see unending rows of books. This is where all the knowledge of the Universe exists…all events, thoughts, words, emotions, intentions that have occurred in the past, present or future of all entities, human and not. I wonder if this is the home for the Akashic Records.

After the North Star visit, we travel east to Egypt, where magic originated centuries before. I am standing in the shifting sands of time. A red carpet appears, and I climb onto it. The carpet whisks me effortlessly through time and space.

I arrive in a city to the west, which appears to look modern-day, maybe Boston, Massachusetts. The Ravens set me down on a cobblestone street with buildings lined up on either side. This place feels the strangest of all! I look at the two Ravens and question, "Why here?" They answer, "You have earned the gifts of Wisdom, Knowledge and Magic. Now you must learn the workings of the Heart."

Raven and Hawk are flying outside my window as I record this journey. I now realize this journey of learning has been about *"the workings of the Heart,"* about realizing my Heart medicine, and to share this Heart medicine with others, whether through in-person therapeutic work or via this book.

CHAPTER 2
Childhood Recollections

The little girl named Cathy,
sometimes called Hopscotch or Little Red Riding Hood by her dad,
was born of a too-young mother and a war-wounded father.
Her parents were told by her baby doctor that she was willful.
She was described as being determined to make things happen,
visiting neighbors when she wanted snacks, asking for cookies,
or stealing plastic flamingos from next door and
hiding them under her mother's clothes-hanging step-box.
She refused to get in the car with her father when he refused
to buy her something at the store and she walked all the way home.
And she answered her mother's evening call to come indoors,
"I'm eating chocolate and watching the moon."

She loved to go to nursery school and do scavenger hunts rather than naps,

followed the bigger kids around,

envied their freedoms and wanted to grow up fast.

She told her mother that if a stranger offered her candy,

she would grab it and run.

She saddled her bike like a horse and rode

as a cowboy with her gun and holster,

yet she was speechless when she met Gene Autry.

Her favorite theme park was Cowboy Town, where she rode the stagecoach

and got robbed by bandits on horseback.

She was so happy to go to kindergarten she told

her mother on the first day of school

that she didn't need her anymore.

She loved to swing high and sing out loud.

And was told by her teacher that she could not take other children's snacks

even if she preferred them over her own,

and that she should not tell stories or tease

the other children at the water fountain.

She was admired for her artwork and

loved to take off without permission,

across busy streets or the railroad tracks to visit her grandma.

She felt bad and different at times because she did not want to play with dolls,

dance ballet or be nice all the time.

Her parents would take her back to the store

to return the candy she had stolen.

She would bribe the kids at the beach for ice cream

in exchange for a phony visit

with her "famous cowboy uncle, Roy Rogers."

She was a member of the clean plate club
and would often want seconds for dessert,
her mom saying no and her dad yes.
Once when she was very sick, her father bought her a checker set
and played with her every day until she got better,
and her mother would sit with her on the bed having well-meaning talks.

She felt her world change at age seven with a move to their new, big house
and the beginning of second grade.
Wildness and imagination became tamed and social acceptance the rule.
A different reality of heaviness and sadness overtook magic and joy.
The world was serious and one needed to please teachers
and behave for mom and dad.
The sting of not being invited to a classmate's birthday party,
but asserting one's pride and showing up anyway to the surprise of the host
and embarrassment of her mother.
She liked to beat the boys at whatever they were doing.
And would daydream of a family of rabbits living
peacefully in a tree trunk.
She would nightdream of a mighty battle between
the Greeks and the Romans
and she would be caught in the middle on marble steps.
Or she would dream of saving her family from a tsunami.

When fifth grade came around,
She was intrigued once more by magic and mystery.
Reading mystery novels became an obsession
along with exploring nearby excavations
with the hopes of finding buried treasure.
She would also sit by a statue of Jesus in the churchyard

hoping to be called by Him to become a nun.
(He never called…thank you, Jesus!)
She loved to play teacher or taxicab driver with her friend Linda,
until her baby brother was born.

His arrival became the greatest pleasure of her life at age nine.
Her first waking thought was to bring the baby to her bed
before her mother got up.
There she would be the mommy and play music and dance with him.
She loved YWCA overnight camp
for the kids, the outdoors and the games,
and did not want to go home.
She hid from her father when he came to pick her up,
but not for long.

She tried not to stir the pot in which anger and grief bubbled
beneath the surface erupting at times
when the man, her father, could not contain
the emotion of broken dreams that seeped out
onto the woman, her mother,
who felt the disappointment in marital "bliss"
and was the target of her husband's rage.
Cathy did what she could
to keep the peace and found solace
in the trees behind her house,
but she wondered why people sacrificed their lives
by getting married
and having children,
especially when it brought such misery.

CHAPTER 3
The Secret of Power

Mom and Dad were at it again. They didn't know I was awake, not safe asleep in my bed. Their voices rising in angry rhythms had moved me from my dreams to the head of the stairs where I could hear what was being said more clearly. Verbal attacks…insults flying…talk of divorce…I became frightened. Visions of my eight-year-old life collapsing. *It couldn't happen! It just wouldn't do!*

When the voices became quiet without resolution, as they often did, I crept back to my room. I prayed to God with fervor, pleading for HIM to *"make something happen to my father, so my mother would love him again!"*

The next morning was St. Patrick's Day. As usual, I accompanied my father to Lenten Mass. However, that day there was a snowstorm, which made getting to Mass nearly impossible. Another car driving in the opposite direction swerved into our lane and hit us head on. It seemed no time had passed when a policeman arrived to help me from the car. I was quite shaken and bleeding profusely from my mouth. My tongue was almost severed! Making my way around the car, I saw my father stretched out on the icy pavement. He looked dead!

I started shrieking, "Daddy, wake up! Daddy, wake up!!" My voice pulled him back into consciousness. Then we were loaded into the ambulance and hurried to the hospital.

After applying a lot of ice on my tongue, the emergency room staff determined I could be released that day, but my father had to stay because of his concussion and broken right knee cap. The doctors told us that tongues are not stitched so I would have to be patient with the healing process of a swollen, sore tongue slit on both sides. My winter coat was so bloodied from my wounded tongue it had to be thrown away right there in the hospital! To this day, my tongue has never completely healed on the left side.

When my mother came to take me home, I saw her talking with my father. As she said goodbye, she leaned over and kissed him. I felt as though a kiss from above had landed on me. I was filled with warm, vibrant energy believing my prayer the night before had played some part in bringing about this scene of repair in their relationship.

For years I remained silent about the pact I had with God, fearing HE would become angry and my power would be lessened if others knew about it. After all, I almost lost my tongue in the accident; a further message to be silent. To me it was clear from this experience that I was special, powerful in some way, and could make things happen. Yet no one around me affirmed or validated this idea of internal authority. The socially sanctioned beliefs of the time were that power was external, and that authorities should rule over us, and dictate the course of our lives. This indoctrination kept me from experiencing my own power any further until I was much older. Only later did I realize the importance of my personal power and that it was my responsibility to exercise it in appropriate ways and speak my truth freely and share it with others to validate and affirm this truth.

CHAPTER 4
Adolescent Reflections

My sister was born when I was eleven years old. At that age I didn't realize a pattern was being repeated. As the eldest daughter, I was suddenly saddled with more household chores and childcare responsibilities after my sister's birth. The same thing had happened to my mother when she was only ten, and her mom had given birth to twin boys. Although barely an adolescent, my father named me godmother for my sister at her Catholic baptism. Certainly an unusual decision. To be given the title of "godmother" was an honor that made me feel proud at the time. This choice speaks to my father's perception of my maturity and personhood, despite my numerical age. Granted, there was not much I could or would decide concerning my sister's religious upbringing, yet the bestowing of this new role indicated my father believed I was ready to be held accountable. My mother's version of holding me accountable was to give me more work, which felt more burdensome than honorable.

My increasing chores meant I didn't search for summer jobs outside the home like other kids my age were doing. Instead my parents hired me to teach my sister and brother. By the time my siblings started elementary school they were far ahead of their peers, already knowing their numbers and letters. While walking my brother and sister for miles in a two-seated stroller, I was frequently asked if I was their mother. I took this at face value as a compliment and didn't notice the irony implied. But I do credit the increased responsibilities with helping me find my voice by sixth grade. I liked being the boss and was unable to keep still. On frequent occasions my teacher silenced me, as my cut tongue had done, yet I was eventually given the task of opening classroom exercises every day for the remainder of the school year.

When puberty arrived, I did not like being one of the tallest in my class and having to wear a bra so early. I wondered if my burgeoning breasts would get in the way of swinging a baseball bat. My changing body brought discomfort and awkwardness I had never felt in my child form. Having been well coordinated and physically adept, I was suddenly unsure of this female body and would have traded it for a male body in a second. But here I was, separated even farther from the freedoms the boys enjoyed. I remember a vivid dream from 7th grade in which a boy snatched my sanitary napkin from underneath my skirt, an odd symbol for my early shame of being stuck in my female form.

In my classes, being told I was smart and headed for a career in creative writing encouraged my feelings of competency. I recall being admired in my red dress with a bandanna and I felt confident whenever wearing it. But overall, the changing relationship between girls and boys in middle school confused me. What was life really about? I often felt lost, as though lacking a compass. My parents were rather strict and did not allow experimentation in any area. I was not allowed to date, do drugs or listen to rock and roll. My free time was controlled by homework and childcare responsibilities and, on occasion, some time with a friend.

High school entry was difficult since my parents pulled me out of public school and put me in a private Catholic day school. I knew no one and cried for a few days, threatening not to return. But I slowly acclimated and became friendly with just about everyone. I was the new kid, who needed to figure things out and be figured out by the others. Most everyone belonged in cliques from their respective Catholic grammar schools, but I managed to stay on the periphery of them all. Without being claimed for membership to any groups, I was free to relate to everyone.

Friendships became more important and dating had begun, but wanting to do well academically was always my first priority. I wanted to have opportunities beyond getting married and having babies. I remember telling stories to get a rise out of folks. And I danced with boys I was not attracted to so as not to hurt their feelings. I joined the basketball culture as a loyal spectator and a player, and identified strongly with my high school clan. But by my senior year I was eager to move on, for college and a larger life.

My natural adolescent development was somewhat curtailed by parental strictness and my responsibilities at home. Because my mother needed my help, it was often a struggle to get permission to be involved with outside work and other activities. Using homework as a pretense, I found consolation and excitement in drawing. Seeing my first Elvis Presley movie inspired me to become an enamored fan. I brought him to life in my drawings and imitated his voice through song. Then I began drawing other characters and cartoons. It seemed I had some talent as well as determination.

My breakout into the larger world came with my acceptance into Mount Holyoke College, which is the oldest of the historic Seven Sisters colleges, an elite group of women's colleges, in the northeastern United States. My father was instrumental in getting me into the right college. My Catholic high school had a meager guidance department, with only Catholic and state college and university catalogs. My dad knew the principal of our local public high school and he managed to get me an appointment with their guidance department to review wider college options. That discussion seeded the idea for Mount Holyoke.

I don't know if my father intended for my college experiences to have such a profound impact on me. Becoming a Mount Holyoke student entirely changed my perception of women. Having never experienced the company of other women of such high intellect and athleticism, I was suddenly the shortest, at 5'8", in this group of females. How I enjoyed living and learning in an all-female environment with brilliant, creative minds — free to explore and develop into me! I could now claim my true identity as a woman with pride.

POEM OF GRATITUDE TO MOUNT HOLYOKE, WRITTEN FOR MY 25TH REUNION IN 1998:

It was a troubled time
my freshman year,
locks of buildings waxed
no access permitted,
Kent State killings
and student strikes,
anti-war slogans
and moratoriums.
Betwixt and between
I was new
to this world
but forced to choose.
Forced to grow up
and think for myself,
lines drawn in the sand
between generations.
Through a complex era, I had landed.

If it were not for
your sweet and magnificent body,
I would not have arrived,
perhaps not even survived.
It was there in your elements
that I sought refuge from the chaos.
You were pure and simple,
grand to the eye and peaceful to touch.
Of all that I was thankful for
during those turbulent times,
it was your grace and steadfastness
that I treasured most.

So I come to visit from time to time
not to pay homage to professors or school fame,
but it is to you, the land,
that serves Mount Holyoke's name,
that I remember
and hold dear to my heart.

Identity this and identity that,
I came here to discover who I am
and now I have come to remind myself of that.
Remembering me in a recent dream
receiving not a diploma in my gown,
but a bow and arrow was handed down.

The idea of being handed a symbolic bow and arrow, instead of a diploma, was a foreshadowing of the coming years, and my exploration of the Divine Feminine and finding my spiritual path. The goddess Diana/Artemis carried bows and arrows. In many literary accounts, arrows represent agency, the ability to reach out (lightning strikes from the heavens), communicate, travel at great speeds (spirit), look forward, and remain true to a purpose and succeed in striking a target (reaching a goal). And finally the ability to soar to reach out to the gods in heaven questing for greater aspirations and deeper meanings.

CHAPTER 5
Bolivia, My Motherland

After finishing my master's degree at the University of Connecticut in Human Development and Family Relations in 1977, with a specialty in Marriage and Family Therapy, I left the United States with my fellow student and romantic partner, Rodrigo. He needed to return to his country, Bolivia, to fulfill his obligation from an OAS scholarship (Organization of American States). At age 26, I was looking forward to an adventure in another country after two intense years in graduate school.

En route to Bolivia, Rodrigo and I traveled by land through Mexico and all of Central America, where the Maya civilization had thrived around A.D. 600-900. I felt a special connection to the Mayan ruins in southern Mexico and Guatemala. Thinking about it now, 45 years later, *I am wonderstruck by how I was partnered with a Latin American man to traverse through lands where I had lived during a past lifetime, as I will describe in a later chapter. It seems my physical presence in this lifetime set the stage for what was to be revealed ten years later about my connection to these Mayan places in a previous lifetime.*

After traveling for many weeks by local buses through Mexico and Central America, Rodrigo and I arrived in Panama. From there we boarded a plane to fly to Cartagena, Colombia, and then on to La Paz, Bolivia, in late fall of 1977. Some call La Paz the Tibet of the Americas.

While landing at the El Alto International Airport I learned it is the highest airport in the world, at 13,327 feet above sea level. With less oxygen in the surrounding air, the environment is a challenge to pilots, who must maneuver carefully in the high-altitude conditions during takeoffs and landings.

After landing, the half-hour taxi ride down to the city was spectacular! As we descended by car from the airport to the city of La Paz, which sits at 11,942 feet above sea level, the evening lights below sparkled like the stars above. The world seemed inverted while we made our way from the darkness of the altiplano (high plain or plateau) into a belly of light.

This landlocked developing world country became a motherland for me; a place of deep nurturing of my internal and external growth. In the cradle of Nuestra Señora de La Paz (Our Lady of Peace), many new aspects took root within me, including a budding awareness of multiple dimensions and the sense of a far longer timeline of world history than I had previously known. And though it would be years before I made the conscious connection, Latin America had once been my home in a previous incarnation.

La Paz was founded upon the ruins of a much older village, previously ruled over by the Peruvian-based Incan empire whose people built Machu Picchu. The Spanish conquistador Captain Alonso de Mendoza defeated the remnants of Incan rule in 1548 and outlawed the use of the Quechua language and culture, but its influences have survived. The resilience of the twenty-five-thousand-year-old indigenous culture in Bolivia rocked my soul when I arrived, gently at first. Even the music seemed both soothing and heartfelt. The songs I heard were about love and death, sung to the accompaniment of "quenas and pinkillas" (flutes), the "sike" (windpipes) and the "charango", a small round guitar.

The indigenous people, the Quechua and Aymara, were friendly but reserved. I had yet to learn about their troubled history, but their clothing delighted my eyes with the brightly colored fabrics and textured weavings. Men wore lightweight trousers and ponchos over their shoulders in a range of vibrant colors, topped off by a *chulla* woolen cap. Women outfitted themselves in multiple layers of skirts, *polleros*, with five petticoats. Silky, frilly blouses, covered with a shawl or "manta," plus a practical apron, and a bowler hat, or *borsalino* as it is called, completed their stylish presentation. These colorfully dressed country people came into the towns to sit in the marketplaces and sell their farm produce. The intensity of the hues of the fresh vegetable displays inspired me to want to learn to cook. And the potatoes…over 200 varieties! First cultivated by the Peruvian and Bolivian native people, some say there are over 10,000 types of "papas." The Europeans had never seen such potatoes until they invaded South America and then they started sending them back to Spain and England by the late 1500s. Bolivians use papas in soups, stews and just about every dish. For the big mid-day meal, they often add beef, pork or chicken.

Rodrigo's family welcomed me, and we often ate our meals together. Despite speaking English too, they encouraged me to speak Spanish. Like Rodrigo, most of his siblings were college-educated and had studied abroad. Discussions were quite lively around the dining table. It didn't matter whether the topic was politics or poetry, everyone had an opinion. I tended to remain silent, since my Spanish was not that sophisticated. I often exchanged smiles with their butler, Felix, with whom I probably was friendliest. The time I spent living with Rodrigo's family was an education in itself.

In a relatively short amount of time, about four months, Rodrigo decided it was best for us to separate. This was not a total surprise. I'd felt him withdrawing from me, offering little access to his thoughts and feelings. He decided to remain in Bolivia and not return to the United States with me, although it took him a while to explain this decision directly. Rather than living abroad again, he chose love and loyalty to his country. At first I could not wrap my head around what he was saying.

"How can you choose your country over our relationship?" I demanded, somewhat naively. He would reply with something like, "I have to break my promise with you to be in service for a greater purpose." This sounded noble but it was still painful to hear. *Had he assumed I would choose our relationship over my own country?* In hindsight, our parting seemed inevitable.

Briefly, we considered staying together in Bolivia, but we both concluded that arrangement would not work. I had just completed my graduate degree, yet I would not be able to work in Bolivia. Not just because my Spanish was not fluent, but because so few professional positions were open to women. Bolivia had many good qualities, which I loved, but the class system kept most Bolivians poor and largely illiterate. I could not imagine losing my professional opportunities and the freedoms I took for granted in the United States. In La Paz, the patriarchs of the families set the rules, and even determined whether the children could travel out of the country. I did not want to live under those social conditions.

During the initial stage of our breakup the cradle of La Paz provided scant comfort. As I looked for another place to live, I felt the hurt, anger, disappointment and deep sadness over the end of my relationship with Rodrigo. But Bolivia had more to discover and experience, so I decided to stay on, rather than return to the States right away. Although Rodrigo had been the central figure in my life those past few years, my independence could be resumed without having to move 4,000 miles away.

Luckily, I found a place to live with Vicky, who was the ex-girlfriend of Rodrigo's friend. An American from Minnesota, she'd chosen not to return to the States. Since completing her service in the Peace Corps, she'd gotten a job directing the language institute where Bolivians learned English and I studied Spanish. A talented abstract painter, and fellow traveler, Vicky became the older sister I'd never had. Living with her stabilized and centered me as I endured the loss of the most significant romantic love relationship in my life until that time.

After settling into my new life at Vicky's, the cradle rocked more gently again, as Bolivia "mothered" me through my emotional stages. I felt loved, appreciated and nurtured in this country, despite the end of my relationship with Rodrigo. For the first time in my life I had no commitments or obligations to anyone else and could just "be" me, for myself. Albeit in my mid-twenties already, after my sheltered upbringing I needed to catch up with some delayed adolescent experiences to reach maturity. Leaving my family and my country allowed me to focus upon myself and my own impressions without interference. In Bolivia I learned, for example, that worthiness and acceptance of others need not be based on credentials and accomplishments but upon the engagement of the heart and being present with others. Bolivia opened my heart, to receive myself, as well as the beauty and rhythms of this ancient culture that prized community and reciprocity.

While in Bolivia I tutored a few students in English, but most of my time was spent reading: Carl Jung, Carlos Castaneda, and the "I Ching." What a luxury! To study what I wanted at my own pace! I kept a dream journal and analyzed my dreams. Often the themes of those dreams concerned the need to protect myself from harm by men. I'd be running away from them, trying to evade capture and imprisonment. In one dream, I was given "cold hardware" to survive. This might have meant receiving weapons, or being rewired internally like upgrading a computer, so I could protect myself. My dreams were not only reflecting my breakup with Rodrigo, but also the instability of Bolivia during the era I lived there. Seeing young soldiers on street corners with rifles was a common sight. Since declaring its independence from Spain in 1825, Bolivia has endured over 190 coups and revolutions, more coups than almost any other country. During my years there from 1977-79, the country was struggling to transition towards democracy. The last known coup attempt was in 1984. Happily it has been relatively stable since then.

Vicky took me hiking around La Paz, and we ventured into other areas, like the Chapare rainforest and the subtropical region of Chulumani. There I enjoyed one of the most peaceful nights ever, sitting in pitch black darkness out on the veranda of our room and enjoying the sight of village fires spread out in the distant hills. Twice we trekked over the Andes Mountains, climbing up to 16,000 feet. Upon our return, we skirted the mountainsides, some covered with sparse vegetation, others with tropical flora or coffee plantations. We often stepped aside to allow llamas laden with meat, wool, leather and other goods to pass us by. The villagers lived in their tiny communities without electricity and running water, yet they possessed some of the world's best mountain vistas!

In addition to my friendship with Vicky, I enjoyed socializing with people from other countries. Many nationals were studying Spanish at the language institute. From a few of them I received a rude awakening about American interventions in other countries. Often conducted under the guise of humanitarian concern, various administrations of the U.S. government removed South and Central American presidents and fomented civil unrest for calculated strategic gains. There were times I was frankly ashamed that my country was responsible for instigating such crimes. I would wonder then, where did I really belong? And which place did I want to call "home"?

But in late 1978, I decided it was time to return to America and move into my professional life. On January 13, 1979, I returned to the U.S. during a blizzard. Trying to land at JFK International Airport in New York was a nightmare. We kept getting diverted while the airplane pitched and rolled in the storm. Many passengers were understandably tense and alarmed in this precarious situation. Although I am not usually relaxed during flights, this time I surrendered to the movement and destiny of this aircraft. I no longer cared whether I lived or died since I felt I'd completed a cycle of life and was thankful for that. I had done a lot, loved much and was fulfilled, so if it was my time to die, I was okay with that fate. It helped that the week before I left Bolivia Rodrigo and I had been together again, this time at Vicky's. She had to travel somewhere that week, so we spent some quality time and found some closure for our relationship. It was bittersweet but wonderful that we had this time together so that I could return "home" with a sense of completion instead of loss.

The plane eventually landed in New York without incident. Then the awkward and somewhat mournful transition back into the American way of life began. I did not expect the re-entry culture shock of returning after living for almost two years in a developing country. It was quite a series of adjustments, from re-learning how to pay for gas at a station, to keeping up at a reasonable speed on the highways, to exchanging American money, being blinded by dazzling lights, and confused by so much noise and so many technological advances.

My family members felt like strangers at first. Communicating and living with them again felt odd, as they had not seen how I had lived. And I had missed what they had experienced in the interim of those two years. Often I felt like a foreigner in my own country for those first few months. I longed to return to the simpler and less congested life I had led in Bolivia, but I needed to refocus and re-adjust quickly since work was starting up in a few weeks. I was asked to teach a course at the university I'd attended, as a substitute teacher, for one of my professors who had taken ill. I had to prepare.

As I now reflect on Bolivia, I learned that the country passed the Law for the Defense of Mother Earth in 2010. It is the world's first law to grant nature equal rights to human rights. This makes it seem even more fitting that Bolivia is where I first felt my connection to the Motherland, *La Ultima Madre*. This law redefines the nation's rich mineral deposits as "blessings." In the face of climate-change challenges, Bolivia is expected to lead the world by setting an example of radical new conservation and social measures to reduce pollution and control the negative effects of industry. And other countries are watching to see if this approach works. The 11 new Rights for Nature include "the right to life and to exist; the right to continue vital cycles and processes free from human alteration; the right to pure water and clean air; the right to balance; the right not to be polluted; and the right to not have cellular structure modified or genetically altered."

A resurgent indigenous Andean spiritual worldview has heavily influenced today's Bolivian legal system. Now it places the environment and the earth deity known as the *Pachamama*, as a living being at the center of all life. The draft of the new law states: "She is sacred, fertile and the source of life that feeds and cares for all living beings in her womb. She is in permanent balance, harmony and communication with the cosmos. She is composed of all ecosystems and living beings, and their self-organization."[4] Indeed, She is.

CHAPTER 6
It Had to Be You

"knew" I had to marry Marvin. Another intuitive nudge, which didn't make logical sense in some ways yet turned out to be for the best. He was raised Jewish, in the Lower East Side of New York City, and came from a lower socioeconomic background. Marvin's father, Max Steinberg, escaped the pogroms in Russia, where he was born, and made his way through Europe to eventually board a ship with other Jews immigrating to the U.S. in 1922 at the age of twelve.

Marvin's mother, Claire, was born in New York City, to parents who immigrated from Russia and Poland.

In contrast, my upbringing was upper middle class, Catholic and suburban, a girl from Connecticut. I was also fifteen years his junior. Both my parents were first-generation Americans; my mother's parents came from Italy and my father's parents from Poland. From my graduate studies, I had learned that people who marry from different socioeconomic backgrounds and religions, and who have wide age discrepancies, are more prone to conflicts, stressors, and divorce. These differences can be serious enough to prevent the chances for satisfying long-term relationships.

Statistically, I understood the deck was stacked against us. Yet we were happily married for almost 40 years. As my husband Marvin would say, "Married for life with hardly no strife."

We met at a job interview for my first postgraduate counseling job in 1979. Having recently returned from Bolivia, I was quite unsettled about who I was, and where I wanted to be at age 28. No longer with the "love of my life" Rodrigo, who remained in his country, I had been through the ending of a romantic relationship and was no longer so naive. Marvin was 42 and single, dating but not settled down, after the traumatic breakup of his marriage ten years earlier. We were not instantly attracted to each other. He resembled Sigmund Freud in appearance and stature. In fact, I remember telling my mother this guy "needed to be shaken up."

Fortunately, I was hired for the counseling position and agreed to weekly supervision of my cases by Marvin. After meeting weekly for a year as he supervised my clinical caseload, I asked him if he had any Yale buddies to introduce me to, who were single and available. Marvin was quiet for a few moments and then said, "I can't do that because I want you for myself."

This did not completely surprise me since there had been some flirtatious behavior between us. My response was, "But you are in a relationship."

"I know," he said, "I will be ending that in time." Some months later, our dating became consistent. We moved in together for a year, then married in 1983 when I was 32 and he was 46.

Once I got to know him, I found Marvin a lot more attractive. He was independent, intelligent, warm, confident and comfortable with himself — a champion of equal rights for women and minorities. He was a deep thinker and effective communicator, and I often thought most women would love to be in a relationship with someone like him because of his abilities to address issues and communicate effectively.

But above all else, he was ALIVE and energized to follow his professional interests, fully engaged with others in his life, and optimistic about most things. Unlike my parents when they were his age, he was not resigned to what life had dealt him and would not give in to disappointment and resentment. I am amazed and proud of how he rose above the challenges of his childhood in a tenement building in the Lower

East Side of New York City, with an anxious mother and depressed, absent father. Despite having no competent role models, and being victimized by street gangs, Marvin was able to complete his doctorate degree in psychology. And he made significant contributions in the field of treatment for compulsive gambling. In 1980, he co-founded the non-profit CCPG, the Connecticut Council on Problem Gambling and served as Executive Director for over 30 years. His accomplishments and awards of recognition are noteworthy. He is most definitely my hero, an example of beating the odds to become more than was ever thought possible.[5]

But Marvin was not a "seeker." He was not interested in any sort of spiritual quest, yet he was interested in hearing about my experiences and actually introduced me to places and venues where I could learn and experience creative, spiritual growth. Marvin introduced me to Block Island, Rhode Island, where we wrote our wedding vows and revisited every year for many years to renew our relationship. He took me to Omega Institute in Rhinebeck, New York, where we took some classes together. I also took Intuitive Training with Ann Armstrong, Drumming with Ubaka Hill, Past Lives Training with Morris Netherton, along with other workshops that were important to my personal and professional development. My husband encouraged me every step of the way.

Through visiting a cousin of Marvin's in Santa Fe, I first went out West to New Mexico. On that trip we went to Taos, where we met Ted Egri, a sculptor. The following summer I apprenticed with him, thanks to Marvin's inquiry and support. Early on in our life as a couple I understood Marvin to be my ally in creative, artistic and spiritual endeavors. While he was not the spiritual partner I wanted in actually sharing those experiences, I came to accept the crucial, supportive role he played in my life. Although Marvin saw himself as an agnostic, I experienced his beautiful spirit and soul in the way he lived life. Fishing was his escape and enjoyment, he said. But I believe rocking on the water soothed his soul and provided the peace others found in prayer or meditation.

One could say I married Marvin for all the reasons cited above, but for me the most compelling reason was my sense that *it had to be*. Whether it was intuition or inner wisdom, it was underscored when Marvin picked our wedding song, "It Had To Be You."

Weeks before I left Bolivia, I'd had a prophetic dream, which I now know know related to Marvin and our future life together: *I was living with my parents at their house and teaching a course at the university. In the backyard, a lion ran toward me. I made a dash for the stairs, but the lion caught up with me and started nuzzling and kissing me. My fear turned into laughter. Then I looked into a room and saw a blond, curly-haired baby boy with blue eyes standing up in a crib.*

In looking at this dream in hindsight, the first part became true immediately, since I needed to stay with my parents until I got a job and could financially provide for myself. Later I learned that Marvin's totem animal was a lion. And the last part — the blond curly-haired baby boy with blue eyes – that turned out to be a premonition of what was yet to come.

The dictionary defines intuition as "the ability to understand something immediately, without the need for conscious reasoning." We all have intuitive capabilities, but some of us develop our intuitive abilities more than most take the time to do. There is training for this and encouragement for trusting this type of inner guidance. Some say intuition is the key to determining which directions one should take in life. This has certainly proven to be true for me and my clients. Others argue in favor of logical reasoning. But our conscious ego minds cannot comprehend things the way our intuitions can. Ideally we would grow up with the ability to rely upon both skill sets, to ensure that we would live to our full potential. Just acknowledging that our inner voices speak our deepest Truth — whether we feel these messages come from our informed gut or our heart — can help our minds relax long enough to appreciate and overcome what our ego defenses and our personalities are conditioned to resist.

In my experience, the universe leaves us clues to help us find our answers if we seek them. Robert Moss, a popular expert on lucid dreaming, points out we have only to pay attention with our senses to discern these directions: to what we are seeing, hearing, smelling, tasting and touching, to discern these directions.[6] These clues and signs are too thought-provoking or emotionally strong to be mere coincidence. The phenomenon of synchronicity is "defined as a meaningful coincidence—an event on the outside that speaks to something on the inside—as opposed to just a random occurrence." It could be as simple as thinking of someone you haven't spoken to in months and suddenly they call you. One time I passed a dead animal on the road and wondered whether it was a wolf or coyote. Just then a car passed me with "Wolf" on its license plate!

If you take the time to set intentions, ask for answers and tune into your environment, you may be surprised with the accuracy of the information revealed to you. There is no substitute for this kind of certainty.

CHAPTER 7
Relationships

I t was never my conscious goal to be married or to have children. As a young girl, I did not dream of marriage, babies and a home because as the eldest, I was already doing so much real caretaking of my younger siblings. Sure, there were fantasies with my attractions to certain men, but I always felt I was meant for more than that. I wanted the freedom to do as I pleased. My dream was to experience as much of life as I could, and to accomplish creative, intellectual and spiritual goals. Perhaps my pursuits were shaped by my parents' curtailed lives. My father, Edmund, never fulfilled his dream of becoming a professional baseball player. Some major league teams in high school pursued him, and he was on track to become a pitcher. Yet WWII intervened. Upon graduation he joined the Merchant Marines and left for Europe. While in France, he lost his leg after stepping on a German landmine. That injury nixed his dreams of playing major league baseball.

I never knew my mother's dreams. Arline did not seem to have an answer when I asked her about them. She wasn't raised with the expectation of following her personal goals, beyond fulfilling those laid out by her immigrant Italian upbringing. As a woman, she faultlessly conformed to the social expectations for women of her era. She had married an older man seven years her senior, and in that sense, our choices were similar. My father was a wounded veteran. In the early years he was able to manage his physical needs without requiring Arline's caretaking as he later would. But she was only 18 when they wed and she never had more than a high school education. Prior to becoming a wife, Arline had been like a second mother to her younger twin brothers. From age ten until her death, Arline was "chief cook and bottle washer." Just shy of her nineteenth birthday, she gave birth to me.

Ed and Arline met in church and were immediately attracted to each other by their respective good looks. They shared the coveted combination of dark hair (almost black) and blue eyes. My father would often say, "Your mother was the prettiest girl in town." And my mother would answer when asked, "Your father was handsome and responsible." Their shared expectations and American middle-class values, of working hard and raising a family, resulted in the births of four children, homeownership and his role as their provider. Their values mirrored those in their families of origin.

My paternal grandparents, Alice and Peter, immigrated as teenagers from Poland in the early 1900's. My father would say he also had Russian and Austrian blood in his veins, since the land boundaries frequently changed in that part of the world, even before his parents were growing up. According to the 1920 U.S. census, our family name, Nogas, was not common in America. We also have a connection to Ukraine. My paternal grandfather Peter took his family to the Ukrainian Catholic Church in Hartford, Connecticut, rather than the Catholic Church in Wethersfield, CT, which was closer to their home. Peter worked as a construction contractor and managed to buy a farm to serve the needs of the growing family he expected to raise with Alice. Unfortunately, in 1928 Peter died of a massive heart attack. He was only in his thirties when he passed. This left his widow, Alice, to raise four boys between three and twelve years of age on her own. My father was the youngest. He remembers jumping on his father's coffin yelling, "Daddy, wake up!" In those days, wakes were customarily held in the family homes before the burial. Alice had the farm, but she had to go out and "scrub floors" in Wethersfield to make ends meet as the Depression arrived.

Dad told me the story of how he skipped kindergarten at age five to stay home and scrub the kitchen floor. When children were absent back then the school nurse would go to the family homes. Seeing my father scrubbing the floor, she asked him why. He told her he didn't want his mother cleaning other people's homes all day only to come home at night and have to clean their house. The nurse was taken aback by this young boy's concern and sense of responsibility toward his mother. But the law said able-bodied children had to be in school. She remedied the situation by having my father attend both morning and afternoon kindergarten sessions. When not expected in the classroom, my father accompanied the nurse to all the school's health classes, where he demonstrated the proper way to wash one's hands, which was a rather distinguished role for a five year old. His being put in a position of leadership from a young age of course made his mother proud!

My mother's parents, Adele and Gus, had also immigrated to the U.S. as teenagers in the early 1900s. They came from the same town, Fossombrone, in northern Italy, but they had yet to meet each other. They were introduced by relatives in Hartford. Gus (short for August) wanted to wed Adele from the moment they first met, but she was not ready to get tied down. First she wanted to experience some independence, although she eventually married him because of his persistence. Adele was the fifth and final child in her family. By the time she was twelve years old her father had passed away, and her mother knew she was dying. Her older children were already out on their own so she decided to take Adele to the Fossombrone convent to be raised by the nuns.

In later years, when Adele would share stories from her six years at the convent, she seemed appreciative of what she learned growing up there. In all of the Rossini family, Adele was known as the culinary artist. Without cookbooks or measuring utensils, she would create the most fabulous meals. She must have learned something in that convent, though they lived in poverty during the First World War. I remember her saying she was delighted to receive an orange at Christmas! When I was young, all five of the Rossini siblings, along with their spouses and children, would convene for Sunday dinner at my grandparents' house. We were too young to fully appreciate Adele's talents in the kitchen. To this day, no Italian restaurants I have visited can match the meals she created. How I miss the homemade pasta and bread, roasted rabbit and lamb, and dandelion salad!

My mother, Arline, Adele's third daughter, was only 48 when the last of her children left home. Ed's multiple health issues became her full-time job until her death freed her from those duties. Arline considered her husband a difficult man. She was often the target of his frustration and anger from his losses and disappointments in life. An abused woman, she would not leave him. I attribute this to her Catholic marital vows, her compassion for his lost leg and her low self-esteem.

Ed lost his three older brothers to ALS (amyotrophic lateral sclerosis), also called Lou Gehrig's disease, when they were in their 50s and 60s. Even though he was the youngest, his brothers turned to him for support and guidance during their lifetimes. Life was not easy for Ed, but he did manage to open a liquor store business that supported his wife and four children. Dad put us all through private liberal arts colleges and was still able to retire in his fifties. Ed was a good father and provider, but he was not the kind of partner my mother was hoping for. Underneath those good looks and his determination to succeed, she had wanted someone to be kind and to care for her. Even though this did not happen, my mother stayed with my father for 58 years, until her death at age 75. I think she expected him to live on "forever," despite his various medical issues. The only acceptable exit for her was to die first.

In 2007, only six weeks after being diagnosed, my mother died of lung cancer. Four months before her official diagnosis she had told my father she did not want to be buried with him or his family. She wanted enough cash to buy her own grave plot in the town where she'd grown up, and where some of her siblings were buried. My father seemed a bit stunned, but he grunted, "Okay," and handed over the money. I think my mother knew she was dying, and this helped her take charge. This was the single self-assertive act I witnessed in my mother's lifetime. Finding marked-up articles about lung cancer, dated six months before her diagnosis, confirmed this when I went through her things after her death.

After she was initially hospitalized, Arline did not want to return to their home to die. She opted to go to a nursing home. I think my mother could not bear the idea of being out of control in her own home, where she had always been in charge. To have strangers taking care of her there was too much to contemplate. She no longer wanted to see my father, and this allowed her to remain separate from him.

I felt my parents were mostly unhappy with each other, yet they did not want to be apart either. It was an unresolved conundrum. I remembered the arguments, verbal attacks and threats of divorce during my childhood. Their behavior raised questions for me about the futility of marital relationships. To be committed to such limiting choices, to put all their time and effort into their children, giving up their own dreams and goals in life, just to have the cycle continue to the next generation? I did not want to be part of that wheel of existence. I wanted my life for myself.

My mother explicitly told me she wanted my life to be different from hers. Mainly she meant not to marry young and get tied down by the kinds of choices she had made. And, to find a man who loved me and treated me well. Yet, I was still groomed by my parents to be a caretaker, just as they were caretakers, in their own respective families. I was held responsible for much of the care of my three younger siblings: a brother three years my junior, another nine years younger, and a sister eleven years younger than myself. Growing up I often dreamt a tsunami was coming, and I had to save my family members before I escaped the wave.

This lifelong struggle, between doing for myself and doing for others, was planted in me by my parents at an age when I was too young to consciously question it, although I became aware of it later. And I did not learn anything about self-esteem and self-love from them because they had martyred themselves for the sake of their family. This was what they had observed others doing around them. And they followed suit, almost on autopilot. No wonder I feared losing myself in having a child.

To help me understand the psychology of self and relationships, I chose courses that focused on these themes in undergraduate and graduate school. My college major was Psychology. And my graduate degree was in Human Development and Family Relations, with a specialty in Marriage and Family Therapy. My own upbringing inspired me to become a marriage and family therapist because I had so much to learn. At various points, I sought out psychotherapy to help me resolve my own issues about family and marital relationships, and whether to have a child. I learned how important it was to make choices that were true to myself, and not the selfless, sacrificial ones my parents had made. While I could be responsible to others, I also had to individuate, and be responsible to myself, primarily. In the healing professions we often say, *"Before healing others, heal thyself."*

Marvin had many of the same beliefs I did about relationships. Fifteen years ahead of me, he had more experience but believed we could be both intimate and independent. Our wedding vows reflected this. Marriage was the ultimate intimacy, yet our closeness would not diminish either partner's individuality. Instead our partnership would strengthen it. Our vows included Kahlil Gibran's lines from "The Prophet":

"Sing and dance together and be joyous, but let each one of you be alone,
Even as the strings of a lute are alone though they quiver with the same music...
And stand together yet not too near together:
For the pillars of the temples stand apart,
And the oak tree and the cypress grow not in each other's shadow."

Thus, we began our marriage, committed to creating a relationship in which each of us could thrive and become our fullest selves.

That path was not always easy. When faced with our conflicts, I often felt the need to flee from my husband. And the demands of raising a child would sorely test my limits. I clearly did not want to relive my mother's caretaker life yet figuring out how to avoid it took some trial and error. During difficult times, I gave myself space. I traveled with a friend, bought something that fed my spirit, or escaped by reading fiction or watching television. The need to reassert my individuality, to be apart and alone, helped me remember who I was, beside the roles of wife, mother and psychotherapist. Those breaks were necessary. Getting back in touch with my real self, feeling like a separate being, with my independent needs and desires, actually helped me stay committed and connected to my marriage and my mothering. This awareness prevented me from feeling consumed by my duties to others. It was a way to retain my identity.

Whether through movement, painting or writing, I learned to give myself regular permission to be creative, to plan time for this and to follow through on my projects. No one else could do these things for me. I had to value myself enough to put my needs first sometimes, rather than be resigned to taking the last piece of toast left on the proverbial tray. By practicing this approach, I learned to remain safely wedded in my primary relationships and still get my needs and everyone else's met, without sacrificing too much. Paradoxically, it was not via my independence but rather through those primary relationships that I learned the most and felt the deepest connections of my life.

CHAPTER 8
The Decision

As I reached my mid-thirties, it was time to make a conscious decision about starting a family with Marvin but I harbored a deep ambivalence about this. I envied those who were clear about what they wanted since I was most definitely unsure. And I didn't know why it was so difficult to make up my mind about having a child. Something so simple, so ordinary for most people, became a complex labyrinth for me.

Luckily my husband, Marvin, was in a similar situation. His sperm had been "damaged" by an untreated varicocele in adolescence, so he had already accepted the idea that procreation might not be in the cards. Knowing this beforehand, I decided to marry him, nevertheless. We would allow fate to dictate whether or not a child would come along to join us.

To explore my indecisiveness, I did some intense psychotherapeutic work. This helped me define what the pros and cons were about having a child. But even becoming an expert in that regard did not make my decision any easier. The ambivalence had a deep hold on me. Thirty-five years after my journey began, and thirty years into motherhood, I can still sense some of that original ambivalence. Although I know more about the reasons for it now, I have never been ambivalent about my son, whom I love beyond words. My questioning was related to how to make this decision. Was it in my best interests to become a mother in this lifetime?

On the purely practical side, I had grappled with an unplanned pregnancy at age twenty-three. That was the first time I faced the decision of whether, or not, to become a mother in this lifetime. At that stage, my intention was to start graduate school in the fall of 1975. By then American women had won the fight to legally terminate unwanted pregnancies, so I would not have to break the law and risk my health. I had briefly dated a Danish man, who was working on an assignment in New York City, but I had gone off birth control some months before while not in a relationship. I knew my body well. My menses came dependably every twenty-eight days, around the time of the new moon. Uncannily, I had the sense that a sperm was connecting with one of my eggs during one of my encounters with the Dane. But I brushed off the odd intuition, assuring myself it couldn't be. I had not realized that I must have ovulated twice that month. When my period was two weeks late, it propelled me to the gynecologist to confirm the fateful news.

When the doctor told me, "You're pregnant," I had the sensation of entering a tunnel where the faint, ringing sound in my ears made concentration difficult. I struggled to stay focused on the here and now. This was most definitely not the news I wanted to hear. I was not ready to be anyone's mother. I did not want to be in this position, much less to be forced to make such a decision. At least abortion was a safe option. A firm believer in women's rights, especially the choices we make about our bodies, I had been active in the women's movement. To help guarantee this freedom, I had marched with women on a national level. But I had yet to deal personally with this dilemma. The issues of reproductive rights and bodily autonomy were no longer abstract.

My choice felt like no choice; to abort was the least bad option. The Danish man did not want to be a father and offered money to help pay for an abortion, plus emotional support, but that would be all. Adoption was not even a consideration. I could not imagine a part of me out in the world, unprotected, another being to be responsible for when I had no control. It boiled down to either keeping my own life, or having no life, if

I brought this child into the world now. In no way did I want to replicate my mother's life. So I chose to keep my own life, as planned.

It was an agonizing wait for two weeks, since I'd been told the embryo was too small for the procedure. Sitting in the waiting room until my turn came, surrounded by women of all races and socioeconomic classes, I could see from our demeanors that none of us wanted to be in this predicament. Yet here we were, each woman needing to end a pregnancy, for reasons of her own. We sat in silence with our thoughts and self-judgments, waiting to be called to the operating room. When the procedure was over, I felt free to pursue my own life again though some negative thoughts and feelings about myself and this decision persisted for quite some time.

A decade later, I was once again in the position of having to decide whether or not to become a mother. This time the decision to try to conceive was prompted by the threat that Marvin might have prostate cancer. We learned this could be a real possibility in early 1985. Despite this news, we departed for our prearranged vacation to Mexico. While there we decided to try to have a baby since we might never have another opportunity. On that trip we conceived our first pregnancy. In the weeks that followed we were delighted to learn that Marvin did not have prostate cancer. Unfortunately, by mid-May that year the pregnancy turned into a fetal demise. And so began our series of five pregnancies and four losses.

That first loss, in 1985, prompted a lot of soul searching and multiple healing experiences, as well as medical tests and procedures. Some of those were invasive, some painful, but all of them indicated the same results. I was physically capable of bearing a child. There was no medical reason preventing me, so we tried again, and again.

Dissatisfied with modern medical reasoning, and ready to consider psychosomatic reasons, I consulted alternative perspectives. Back in my twenties, an astrologer had read my chart and told me there was "a small window of opportunity" during which I could conceive and have a child. Although I took these things with a proverbial grain of salt, I kept an open mind seeking answers to address my ambivalence. Psychics told me having a child was not necessary for my soul in this lifetime. The choice was mine, along with the choice of whether or not to believe what any psychic said. I always used my own intuition to filter their messages.

An esteemed international spiritual leader told me a soul was "waiting on the wing." And another said, a soul would "keep trying to return," but I had to make myself ready. Intellectually I knew I could manage a child and the rest of my life, yet I held on to these kernels and clues. As we endured each successive loss, I tried to gain some deeper understanding of myself and the mysteries of life. Marvin and I discussed whether we should cut our losses and quit or stay the course. But each loss only made us more determined to try again. A friend confided, "You will experience a depth and capacity to love like no other when you have a child." That intrigued me. Although I was still ambivalent, I did not want to miss out on something so rich.

The most powerful of all these healing experiences was a past life regression I had with Dr. Netherton, which I will share in the next chapter. This finally helped me comprehend something profound about the origins of my fears. They were remnants of events from another lifetime. What had happened in that past incarnation had caused me to equate childbirth with my death.

The past life facilitator, Dr. Netherton, explained to our group "the experience in the womb and birthing canal becomes the index of life's experiences for the person being born." In addition to triggering karmic resolutions from a past life, my experiences of being born also brought up fears of dying when giving birth.

I asked my mother about her experience when I was born. She was young when she had me, her first child, ten days before her nineteenth birthday. When she went into labor, they gave her something for the pain. The medicine made her irrational. Seeing knives on the table she became fearful the doctor was going to cut her belly open; she had to be restrained. This is another connection with what I was shown during my past life regression. It also revealed karmic ties between Marvin, me and an unborn child.

CHAPTER 9
In Another Lifetime

The ropes are cutting into my wrists and ankles. They will come for me soon. I cannot believe this is happening to me. Only a short time ago my existence was pure bliss. A dream life for a young girl, living in a palace, every wish granted, any desire fulfilled. Only now do I realize why they were so keen to pamper me. I am about to be sacrificed against my will.

No one told me why I was chosen. They came to our home when I was nine years old. Everyone was so nice then. They made me feel special about being selected. Their attempts to make everything so perfect kept me from asking any questions. Saying goodbye to my parents had been the hardest part, knowing we would never see each other again. Yet through their tears they assured me this was a great honor for our family. I was doing something that would make our name eternally glorious. The promise of a new life sounded so wonderful that our parting seemed to be sweet sorrow.

In the palace, I slowly came to understand from the whisperings of the maid servants that I was being groomed to bear the seed of the High Priest in our region. Four glorious years and now all that has come to pass.

Being raised in this Holy Place prepared me to carry the salvation of our people. Once my monthly flow began, my days were measured so I could become the receptacle for our leader's sanctified sperm.

Many months passed before it was my turn to be impregnated with his holy seed. I was taken to a special room in the palace filled with the fragrance of Flor de Mayo. These sacred flowers, along with the bitter drink of cacao and herbs, prepared me for the sexual act with the High Priest. I don't remember much while it was happening since I separated from my body for the duration of the activity. Sometimes I would have to lie there for hours to make sure the sacred semen did not go to waste. When the effects of the elixir wore off, I would feel a dull pain in my pelvic area for a few days, until the next month when we would repeat the same ritual coupling. After conceiving, I was worshiped as no other, and made to feel the Highest Mother of all.

Because I was barely thirteen, there was concern that my birth canal would be too immature for the baby to pass. If the infant died, it would all be for naught. Only a live child was a proper sacrifice to our gods, Chac, who ruled over the rain for our crops, and K'awiil, who gave us sustenance to survive. Ix Chel would be called in since she was the goddess of medicine and childbirth and would make sure the infant's heart would still be beating for the sacrifice.[7] The decision was made by the High Priest to cut my belly open so the infant could be safely removed before it became too large. Once I fully comprehended this was about to happen, I was terrified.

I wanted MY baby. No one should take my child from me. I didn't care anymore about the sacrifice or doing what everyone else said was right. The others were astonished. How could I resist what was to be? No one's personal needs could be put above our people's lives! Wasn't I grateful to be the chosen one? They reminded me, "You should be honored and go willingly, or else it will spoil this gift to the gods."

I can hear their sandals slapping the polished floor tiles in the passageway. They are coming now to take me to the High Stone Altar. I struggle and scream "NOOOOOOOO!" I flail my arms and thrash out. But they are stronger than I. Where are the women? Only men do I see. Why have they deserted me? Do they know the pain of giving up their own?

CHAPTER 9

The men wrestle me down onto the stone slab. The High Priest, void of emotion, takes the knife and makes a vertical slit across my swollen belly. Blood gushes forth and I go numb with the pain. The people cry out words of redemption as the sacrificial babe is held up to be admired by all.

I try to reach for him, to grab him back and shield him with my body. I scream out with my last bit of strength, "GIVE ME BACK MY BABY!!!" One look and my hand curling around his little fingers that clung to mine was all that was allowed before he was pulled away from me forever. My unspoken words flew to him, telling him we would meet again, soon. The resounding noise in my head is lost as the throng pushes on with its young victim to be slain. My eyes lock onto the full moon at its zenith as life blood spills on the ground and I am left for naught.

Suddenly my attention switches back to the present day. I am in a classroom at the Omega Institute in Rhinebeck, New York. It is 1986. This past life drama has been facilitated by Dr. Morris Netherton, whose familiar voice whispers, prodding me, "Who is the High Priest? Look at his face!"

"I can't!" I cry, "I won't!"

The voice pushes me on, "Look, NOW, and see…"

I take one look and see the high forehead and I know who this man is. I sob out, "It's my husband!"

The voice says gently, "Open your eyes and behold this man."

My eyes open and lock with Marvin's. His eyes hold the pain and anguish of new awareness about this past life journey we have shared together. We cradle each other and softly rock as our tears flow and heal what was torn asunder.

It is here that hope rises so we can begin again.

Past Lives Therapy is a powerful tool. It provided me answers I could not find in Western medicine about why I was losing so many pregnancies. Healing unresolved wounds from past lives put my mind to rest in a way nothing else had. Dr. Morris Netherton was the Founder and President of the Association for the Alignment of Past Life Experience. Now deceased, his past life therapy methods continue to be practiced by Dr. Thomas Paul at the Past Life Regression Center in Los Angeles, California, which had been co-founded with Dr. Netherton.

After this past life regression, I did some research about infant sacrificial rituals. Many cultures, particularly that of the Maya, participated in child sacrifices, hoping to please or appease supernatural beings. Babies were considered the purest form of offering and parents gladly gave their children up for this dubious privilege. Young girls were taken from their parents and raised to be sacrificial surrogates. They were well treated while being prepared, given an excellent diet, and a feast in their honor, before being ritually killed.[8,9]

My firsthand experiences convinced me to believe in karma. Because of prior life events, we may find ourselves in perplexing relationships. We can believe in reincarnation, or not, but I have found no better explanation that makes sense of the patterns I have witnessed, after observing myself in another existence. Older spiritual teachings include the idea that before this present incarnation we chose the people we are with in order to work through the struggles we inherited. Many traditions imply there are no accidents. Whether we need to bring closure to unresolved past life issues, or we need to learn specific lessons about ourselves by relating to others, it is said that souls choose to return to Earth to have these opportunities. Yes, some of these relationships are painful, and we suffer loss, but this is why we came here: to love, learn and fully grow. My mother, for example, did she require a dire situation, like her impending death, to experience what it is like to stand up for herself? "I didn't assert myself through life, but I will dictate what happens when I die."

In working with couples over the years, I have found some cannot live with, or without, each other. There is constant drama. They push each other's buttons, acting out, projecting onto each other the inner dynamics they need to own and work through themselves. When these couples finally get to the underpinnings of what is triggering each of them, and take responsibility for their own work, sometimes there is resolution and the relationship prospers. Other times they realize they no longer need to be with that partner and the relationship ends.

Relationships contain the possibilities of working through earlier life lessons, such as those with parents or authority figures, as well as our past life relationships. These can widen our perceptions of who we are in the largest sense. And likewise, we are assisting others to understand who they are, so each of us gets to experience the range of opportunities that help us develop into more complete human beings and companion souls.

CHAPTER 10
The Trial and Error Journey

After the past life experience, our healing journey continued. And so did our pregnancy losses. Despite Marvin's low sperm count, I kept getting pregnant. Each loss was for a different reason, which I will share in this chapter as the lessons may be of value to others. In trying to make sense of all these losses, what came to mind was the theme of sacred reciprocity. There has to be an exchange. Something must be given in order to make room to receive. As mentioned in the previous chapter, indigenous peoples had practiced child sacrifice, and in European fairy tales like Rumpelstiltskin, a baby is handed over in exchange for something valuable.

Although I was not *consciously* making offerings of my pregnancies, perhaps some underlying need to give and receive was a subconscious factor in my efforts to heal myself and achieve my goal of a full-term pregnancy and live birth. Dr. Lissa Rankin writes about the practice of making offerings as part of a healing journey.[10] And pagan traditions, like those of the Druids, made regular offerings to connect with spirits in nature and other realms. In Buddhism, symbolic offerings are made to the Triple Gem, giving rise to contemplative gratitude and inspiration. Many religious groups request monetary donations in exchange for blessings and guidance, so these are not uncommon expectations.

Part of my personal spiritual practice includes honoring the four elements that keep us alive and in balance, so it made sense to me that my pregnancy losses could be considered as offerings to Air, Fire, Earth and Water. In Greek mythology, and others, these elements are often ruled by goddesses.

I consecrated our first loss in 1985 to the goddess of Air, Hera, known for protecting women during childbirth. This had been my first experience giving birth. An amniocentesis test at twelve weeks revealed the fetus was male and suffering from hydrocephalus, a fluid buildup in the brain. The fluid was made too quickly to be absorbed into the bloodstream. The excess fluid caused the head to enlarge, increasing pressure around the brain. This abnormality threatened the baby's survival. Doctors advised us the fetus would most likely die. And we decided to allow nature to take its course rather than abort.

During this time, I prayed daily with Spirit and the baby, wishing it freedom from suffering and giving it permission to leave. I also invited it to return, if and when the time was right. In a matter of weeks this little being took its leave. To release the deceased fetus, I was given Pitocin, to induce contractions. That was an awful experience; but given the circumstances, it went as well as could be expected. While Marvin and I grieved this loss, test results assured us this abnormality was not caused by any genetic defect. It was unlikely to occur again. The advice was to keep on trying.

Our second pregnancy ended in a miscarriage, at about eight weeks, in 1986. This occurred after a trip to Kilauea volcano on the Big Island of Hawaii. While nothing physically extraordinary happened on that trip, I had felt a connection to the goddess Pele, ruler of Fire, Wind and lightning. The thought entered my mind that this baby was a sacrifice to Pele.

Some months later in 1986, I became pregnant again. This third pregnancy also ended in an early miscarriage, after a camping trip to the White Mountains in New Hampshire. Before that sad event, I remembered feeling connected to Gaia, Mother Earth energy and Earth goddess, while lying on the ground nodding off to sleep. After the loss I wondered if this baby was an offering to Gaia. The only medical explanation given for this loss was the possibility of my progesterone being low. If I got pregnant again, taking progesterone was recommended.

Marvin and I were hopeful when we got pregnant the fourth time in 1988. I took the recommended hormone treatment and reached sixteen weeks when the amniocentesis test could be done. The results were all normal. We learned our baby was female and we named her Tara. I believed in trying to develop a relationship with children before their birth. Tara means "star" and "protection/salvation from difficult situations" according to what I was able to learn from various spiritual traditions.

A few weeks later, however, while on a smooth 45-minute ferry ride from Point Judith, Rhode Island to Block Island, some amniotic fluid started to seep out. When I saw my gynecologist, he said my membranes had ruptured for no apparent reason. I was hospitalized at Yale New Haven Hospital, with my hips up in the air, in an effort to prolong the pregnancy. If the baby could reach twenty-two weeks in utero, there was a better chance of a healthy birth, with fewer complications. If Tara was born now, at nineteen weeks, she would not survive.

The wait was agonizing. Would Tara become a reality in our lives? Every day the ultrasound revealed a healthy-looking baby with enough amniotic fluid to survive. The dilemma was how long I could remain in this condition, without developing an infection after the rupture. If I got an infection, they would have to induce me, since the risk was high that I could die. If Tara came early and survived, as a preemie she might have life-threatening complications. It was recommended I abort her, to avoid both of those possibilities. Many weighed in on this decision, medically and otherwise, but I chose not to end Tara's life. We had already connected and I was hoping for a positive resolution.

But we don't always know what the highest good might be for all concerned. In a cruel twist of fate, within a few hours after I told everyone about my decision to stay the course, my body revolted. A massive infection took hold so quickly I hardly knew what was happening. My involuntary shaking and high fever alerted everyone that I was going into shock. I was prepped for delivery, given high doses of drugs, along with IV antibiotics. I remember shaking so much it was difficult to get the IV line into me. It seemed to take forever, but after a few hours, Tara was delivered vaginally. At twenty and a half weeks, she weighed only one pound. Since her lungs were too underdeveloped, she did not live for long. All the decisions we had agonized over were taken away from me. Tara left us on July 29, 1988. In line with the other losses, I found some comfort from the thought that another of my babies had gone to a goddess. This time of the sea, Amphitrite. I later found out that Tara is sometimes referred to as a sea goddess.

After Tara's arrival came the oddest moment. She was handed to me, to hold for a photo. This is routinely done after a baby is delivered but I was dazed and distraught. I did not know if I wanted this, or not, but it happened anyway. She was so small she fit into the palm of my hand. Tara never opened her eyes or mouth, but there was a slight movement around her eyes…maybe she winced. I kept this photo, along with the urn of her ashes, but was never sure where to put it. Photo albums contain visual histories of people and places in one's life, but this was a single photo, which would have no before and no after, no continuity. It remains a photo without an album.

Marvin described the loss of Tara as a "kick in the teeth." All seemed to be going so well with the pregnancy. Hadn't we already paid our dues with the losses that preceded it? Marvin's mother, Claire, had died a month earlier believing we were going to have a little girl. We were devastated. Neither of us wanted to consider trying to get pregnant again for at least a year. This fourth loss would take a while to recover from. The medical professionals kept reassuring us each loss was a "fluke" of nature. From their perspective, we had what it took to make a baby, and have it survive.

In 1990, two years after losing Tara, we decided to try one more time. We consulted an esteemed infertility expert to make sure we were covering everything possible to have a successful outcome. After months of testing and collecting data, the expert delivered his findings to us. "You have no chance of having your own baby."

Looking at me, he said, "We would need to laser apart your heart-shaped uterus but," as he glanced toward my husband he added, "you have no sperm at all at this point, so why bother doing any procedures, unless you decide to use someone else's sperm? I must go see my next patient. Good day."

Marvin and I sat stunned with this news, especially hurt by the brusque and insensitive way it was delivered. After all we had invested — time, energy and money — to be so callously treated was beyond our comprehension. In disbelief I turned to my husband and said, "Can you believe this guy delivers the most sensitive and intimate information to people who are in pain about their inability to get pregnant? Thank goodness we are both therapists and can process this incident with each other. I don't know how others deal with this distress and suffering without an empathic doctor."

Marvin nodded in agreement, but I could see he had already begun to mourn the child that was never to be. We held each other as tears were shed, but some part of me felt relief. After five years of trying to have a child, I could now move forward with my life. It was time to close this chapter.

But once again fate had other plans. A month before that last visit to the infertility expert, my friend and work partner, Wendy, joined me to travel in the southwest and visit sacred places. The last of our destinations was Chaco Canyon in New Mexico. We arrived late in the evening, in full darkness. After 40 miles of slow driving on rutted dirt roads we were greeted by a "Campground is Full" sign. Not to be deterred by the late hour, poor road conditions and nowhere else to stay for many miles, we continued to circle the campground. *Something inside told me we were meant to be here and that we would find a place to sleep.*

We spied a vacant spot, although the site was reserved by a name. We decided to pitch our tent anyway and settle in for the night. If someone showed up, we hoped they would understand our plight and share the space with us. Thankfully, no one showed up, and we slept through the night undisturbed.

In the morning, we explored an ancient ruin. After a while, I found a large slab lying upon some other stones. Something instructed me to lie upon this stone slab, so I did. I have no memory of what happened during the next half hour. I wasn't sleeping nor was I in my usual waking state.

Later that day, visitors were asked to leave Chaco. Apparently the federal government had not yet voted on funding for national park employees, so Chaco and the other parks had to close. Our visit was brief, but the timing was exact, and the impact of my experience there would be revealed in the coming weeks.

In a few days, Wendy and I wrapped up our travels and returned to our respective homes. Unbeknownst to Marvin and me, baby number five was conceived during the following week. This was the week before the infertility expert informed us we had zero chance of conceiving with

Marvin's sperm. Two weeks later my menses was late, and the pregnancy test proved positive. We were actually pregnant at the last meeting with that infertility expert! So much for their conclusive testing!

I have heard many other stories like this, which leads me to believe fertility medicine alone does not make babies happen. At the very best, some procedures can make our bodies ready to become pregnant. But the actual energies of sperm and eggs, and why they choose each other to form another life, is a mystery we'll never fully comprehend. Yet we may glimpse enough of the invisible powers to find the help we need to facilitate our healing.

A couple of months afterwards, I found a book about Chaco Canyon's history.[11] It told of the Anasazi, or "ancient ones," who populated the San Juan Basin, parts of Utah, southern Colorado, Arizona and most of New Mexico. Evidence discovered in the canyon proves these people created an ingenious, large-scale, urban technological society hundreds of years ago. Their culture centered around elaborate rituals, monumental buildings, unity consciousness and principles of peace.

After a 700-year reign, the Anasazi mysteriously disappeared. We now know the Zuni and Hopi are their descendants. Anasazi is a Navajo term for "ancient enemies." Pueblo peoples of New Mexico do not wish to refer to their ancestors in such a disrespectful manner, so they are known today as Ancestral Puebloans. Some refer to Chaco Canyon as the site of an ancient Amerindian Mystery School, and a good place to seek the wisdom of the ancestors in their powerful sacred land.

I also learned the ruin we chose to visit by chance, Pueblo Bonito, contains four kivas used only by women. Kivas are round circular spaces used primarily for ritual purposes. Women met in these kivas to perform ceremonies to help with fertility!

The stone slab that "called" me was near those kivas. The book also described the guardian spirits of the canyon and their willingness "to assist the Earth and all its creatures into a new era of hope and unprecedented human possibilities." *My sense of this experience was that invisible forces helped me to conceive Aaron.* While the physical conception of our son with Marvin occurred immediately after this trip, I believe the spiritual conception took place in Chaco Canyon.

Despite all our scientific advances, even in fertility treatments, conception remains beyond our control. Perhaps Spirit has a hand in this and directs the lifeforce of its own accord, for hard to fathom reasons.

Several years ago a client came to me because she was struggling to conceive a child via donor sperm. She already had two children from a sperm donor and wanted a third. Yet after several tries the procedure was unsuccessful. My client was having difficulty accepting she would be the mother of only two children since she had a strong, prophetic vision of herself as a mother of three children. After some therapeutic work, she came to a place of acceptance with the way things were. Some years later, I received a Christmas card from her, with a photo of three children. Her note said after twenty years of not conceiving with her husband, they had produced a biological child of their own; the third child in her prophetic vision!

CHAPTER 11
A Glorious Culmination

The silver lining inside my dark journey through pregnancy losses was the unfolding of my spiritual path. Each miscarriage spurred my quest to understand why and find the meanings within these devastating events. As each door closed with the loss of each potential new life, another door opened. If not for those losses, we would not have had these experiences. Again, the idea was to accept the loss, as an offering, one thing given before something else could be gained in its place.

Perhaps Tara left because at that time my task was to mature, to birth more of myself. For example, the timing of Tara's departure created the opening for a formative visit to New Mexico later that summer. This led to an introduction to the sculptor Ted Egri. By the following summer I was studying sculpture with him as an apprentice, learning about forms and reshaping my life.

I fell in love with Taos. Its magical energies reawakened my right brain, feminine side, affirming my creativity and spirituality. That summer of 1989 reconnected me with my deepest longings, my desire for creative fulfillment, as a mother and an artist. Over the years this relationship has grown. I cannot imagine life without spending some time each year in New Mexico. The very land and wind recharge my spirit. "The Land of Enchantment" as they call it, has given me many sacred experiences. In return, I bring others to this special place to be inspired too, offering workshops and retreats from my home there.

Accepting all our losses, going through the past life realizations and making this connection to New Mexico combined to somehow transform us. We lived with less worry and stress. Generally speaking, our fifth and final pregnancy (1990-91) went well. I restricted my travel and took more rest than recommended. Along with these precautions, my gynecologist stitched my cervix shut at twelve weeks to prevent my membranes from opening. It went unspoken that this attempt was it, our last effort to have a child. I would be forty and Marvin fifty-four when this baby was born. I recalled what the astrologer told me in my twenties, "There is only a small window of opportunity."

A few months before the baby was due, I told my doctor I preferred to have a cesarean birth. Marvin and I had discussed this. Having come this far we did not want to take any extra chances with a vaginal birth. We wanted the baby to be lifted out. Oddly, I see this as additional proof of healing from my former lifetime because I no longer had any fear of my belly being opened to remove my child.

But my gynecologist knew none of that. He said this was not an elective procedure. Cesareans were only performed when medically necessary. He explained what would have to happen, should a cesarean birth be called for, indirectly educating me. Fortunately, Aaron had other ideas. He turned breech, head up, arriving about a month before his due date. *He must have been listening.* Because of our close relationship with my doctor, and his previous experiences with our losses, we chose the July date he would be available for surgery. It was two weeks before Aaron's actual due date, but he was already a big baby.

On July 11, 1991, Aaron Taos Steinberg was born healthy at 11:43 am, and we were greatly relieved. He weighed eight pounds and three and a half ounces, was 20 ½ inches long, with deep blue eyes and strawberry blond hair. The premonition I had in Bolivia all those years ago came true!

Some believe babies born breech, or in the caul, are natural healers. And on the day Aaron was born there was a total solar eclipse. I paid close attention to all the signs, both celestial and mundane. Apparently the magnitude of this eclipse was greater than any since the sixth century. And there won't be another like it for eight hundred years.

Astrologists claim being born during the time of a solar eclipse means a baby is destined for greatness and sprinkled with a little extra pixie dust. Of course I'd like to believe this. Perhaps this pixie dust is the collective energy of our unconscious global aspirations, seeking to be actively expressed upon the Earth. According to Karen McCoy, evolved souls born during solar eclipses are returning to help foster our planetary growth and development.[12] This sort of information made me wonder about the destiny of our child.

Marvin chose the name Aaron because it was his middle name, given to him by his mother, who thought it was "beautiful." Aaron was the first high priest of the Israelites, and the word means "lofty, exalted high mountain" in Hebrew. I chose Taos for Aaron's middle name, because Taos, New Mexico, had fostered my creativity and spirituality. The Tao(s) also means the way, the natural order of the universe, in Eastern philosophy and spiritual practices.

After our seven-year ordeal, Marvin and I were absolutely overcome with joy to be a family of three. My body could finally rest and re-stabilize, after the nearly constant hormonal and weight shifts during this period in my life. Now we could settle into life together, to explore all our connections.

Many stories of infertility and pregnancy loss do not end like this with a live, healthy birth. Although I'm grateful my journey ended positively, my heart goes out to those who may not yet know the endings of their pregnancy stories. For seven years I dealt with the serial pain of multiple pregnancy losses. This forced me to educate myself and to find creative ways to keep going and keep healing spiritually, emotionally, physically and psychologically. Those lessons formed the basis of this book.

Twenty-three million miscarriages occur in this world every year. Most would-be mothers suffer through them in silence. And one in every three of those women are at risk of developing post-traumatic stress disorder, anxiety and depression.[13] We need more stories from these women, and the people who love them, to help us understand these challenges so it is easier to cope with them. Anyone struggling with pregnancy and fertility difficulties knows how trying it is to *not* know. This particular kind of ambiguity, and learning to accept what is *not* to be, can push us to the brink of our capabilities especially when we face these situations more than once.

Couples' relationships also suffer from pregnancy losses and fertility difficulties. "Married or cohabitating couples who had a miscarriage were 22 percent more likely to break up as opposed to couples who had a healthy baby at term. For couples who had a stillbirth, this number was even higher, with 40 percent of couples ultimately ending their relationship."[14]

After four unsuccessful pregnancies, I became well acquainted with the depth of despair that motivates one to seek answers beyond those offered by the modern medical establishment. If recounting my experiences provides any comfort to my readers, I hope you will also feel encouraged to find explanations of your own. Balance the limits of intellectual logic by exploring intuitive realms of knowing. And seize the opportunities to express your love and creativity in new ways. The world needs all sorts of nurturing and feminine wisdom. All is not lost when so many crave mothering and connection. I like to think the Great Mother depends upon us, Her human helpers, to deliver what is needed, when it's needed, wherever it is needed. We just have to respond in the moment. Knowing such stories beforehand reminds us to open ourselves up, when we least want to, after a great loss. There are many sources of love. Receive from as many of them as you can.

If we refuse to reach out, we risk losing our sanity. Even though Marvin and I chose to get pregnant five times, we knew we could not control the consequences. Our human choices cannot guarantee our preferred outcomes. It's what we do next that matters. When facing forces beyond our command, we must be able to accept that other factors are involved which we may not comprehend. I've been told, for instance, that our souls make sacred contracts, in the spirit world, before we re-enter Earth's physical realm. Apparently some of us have soul groups we incarnate with more than once. When we have a sense of déjà vu, in a certain place, or with someone we just met, pay attention. Ask your intuition and dreams for additional information and clarification. Try past life regression work. Find the answers you need.

Since we already covered the karma between couples, I just want to add that some believe our children choose us to be their parents. In a past life, we might have been their children. And this time around the roles, or even the genders, are reversed. Try to imagine why your children chose you. And why you might have chosen your parents. This is not to excuse or explain away abuse, but to restore your sense of power and choice. Perhaps an investigation of past lives can clear up some confusion, as mine did, when I discovered the root cause of my prior ambivalence about motherhood.

After the loss of our first pregnancy a prominent psychic told me that Spirit had left because "you and Marvin were not ready for him. You need to communicate more and listen to each other." When she said this I laughed because we were both therapists. And we were supposed to be good communicators. Yet there was some truth to her statement. Both of us were busy with our professional lives. We were not prioritizing quality time with each other. How unusual and amusing that our unborn child was already giving us feedback. The psychic said this entity, whom we called Aaron, was still determined to join us. He would keep trying, just like Douglas MacArthur. "I shall return."

Another psychic had told us there was "a babe on the wing" waiting for the situation "to be ripe." Psychics know the power of suggestibility. So everything they say we must consider with discernment, but I let myself imagine this entity Aaron might want to have us as parents. Shifting my perspective prevented my thinking from falling into a rut of negativity. Did my other pregnancy losses have anything to do with those entities changing their intentions? Perhaps. For whatever reasons they were not ready to incarnate. Why did baby number four, Tara, decide to leave after I made the commitment to have her, no matter the handicaps she might have?

I'll never know for sure. But pondering wider possibilities stretched my mind a bit more. While in our human forms, we can only make sense of things with the skills and resources we have at our disposal. Some may not be interested in alternative perspectives from providers such as psychics, healers, spiritual teachers, past life facilitators, astrologers and naturopaths. And that's okay. But this integrated approach did work best for us. We did not rule out modern medicine, we fully incorporated its advances, but we also had faith in other approaches too. Our story may be most useful to those who are curious to explore alternative methods.

CHAPTER 12
The Way of the Child

In the early years of raising Aaron, I did my best to listen and observe to understand what he needed from me. Yes, I read all the books and knew what to expect at each stage of development, but I waited for signs directly from him. There is no one right way to raise a child. Parents who raise more than one know this. As the older mother of a single child I had the time and the intentions to respect and support my son's way of being in the world. In return, Aaron taught me much.

"Thanks for having me, Mommy," said my nearly
two-year-old son, Aaron Taos, as I changed his diaper.

I gasped and stood back a moment.

Did I hear him correctly? I believe I did.

How could this small being utter such a profound statement
of gratitude and understanding?
Did he know I lost four babies prior to having him?
That his father had barely enough sperm to conceive them
and was told there was none left to create him?
Did he know of our deep pain and sorrow at losing a daughter
so soon after her premature birth?
What else did this little soul know?

After his expression of gratitude, I was convinced Aaron knew, on some level, of our journey to bring him into being. On occasions, when distressed, I remember his arms encircling me on his own initiative. His embrace is full of love, a love so pure of heart and soul all within me is healed. And I beam it back upon him with gratitude.

Those experiences made me wonder what more was in store for Aaron and me, as his mother. Children hold their own soul information. Unless outside forces interfere, they know how to connect to their own source of innate knowledge. Well-meaning adults tend to teach their children what is socially acceptable from their sense of the world. But this can disrupt the natural process of the child's development. Adults usually operate with an inherited set of criteria learned when they were conditioned to function in society. In turn they impose these values on the child, but our children will not be living in our pasts. They will inhabit a very different future. Generation after generation repeats socially sanctioned learning, which prioritizes logic and mental processes, instead of developing instinctual knowledge and the innate wisdom that comes from the body. Conditioned by the adult world, children become estranged from their own gifts, from their own natural rhythms and deepest ways of being. The adult world experiences have their value, but so does the world of the child. Remembering and reclaiming our own inner lives and intuitive wisdom helps us support the same in our children.

Our inner child knows we are connected to all things, visible and invisible. We can relate to all these things more easily when we believe everything is alive. Reducing the world to animate and inanimate objects, categorizing species, labeling molecules and atoms can dull the awe and wonder we once enjoyed. I recall how Aaron reminded me of the connection to the magical. He must have been around nine months old and beginning to walk. He was excited, pointing at the moon as I walked into the room. "Mama…moon!" This was one of his first words after dada, mama and truck.

We grownups often forget how amazing the Universe is. With our work blinders on we lose our opportunities to relate to the whole smorgasbord of everything before us. One of the best things our children do is to remind us of Nature and how to rediscover our joy in everything. The smallest items, a fly or a pebble, can become a source of connection and something to tell stories about.

Children are most alive when outdoors and relating to animals. Open channels for Nature's energies, they absorb much of Her light and rejuvenating properties. Kinship with animals, pets or the wild things who operate from instinctual drives, bring squeals of delight and excitement.

For example, as a preschooler, Aaron collected numerous rubber replicas of dinosaurs and other creatures. He would line them up, or move them in circles, often having them face off with each other. Then he would become a cheetah, and move on all fours, racing through the house. His speed and dexterity astonished all witnesses. Many times, I experienced his feline energy coming from behind me, and would yelp when he pounced. In later years, at a high school soccer practice, his coach gave the players a drill to run on all fours across the field. They all marveled at how quickly and easily Aaron performed this feat!

Children move towards whatever calls forth their energy. They become fully alive when engaged in this dynamic process. Once in their natural flow, with whatever sparks their energy, they like to stay with it. When interrupted or pulled away they become upset, understandably. Even adults enjoy uninterrupted activities when we are focused. Children thrive in the process of play when they are fully in concert with what is happening and what they are doing. They need to feel this freedom to be themselves and do what is healthy and harmonious in the moment. Using their entire bodies, they are also developing new skills and improving their abilities simultaneously.

They often take on the characteristics of the animal or person they are imitating. This merging is a form of creative enactment. It allows them to act out all the characteristics they notice in the desired person, animal or object, so they recreate it internally. As parents we mirror this activity, consciously or unconsciously. I remember an afternoon when I felt spontaneous and creative during a fun interaction with my son.

"OH MOMMY!" exclaimed Aaron as he came through the door from kindergarten. His eyes were wide in astonishment as he saw me painting on a five-foot canvas, squeezed into our six-foot-square kitchen. Our eyes flashed with excitement and laughter at this spectacle. This was my first painting in twenty years. My son had yet to see this side of me. Later I thought, "Dare I become more than a mother, Aaron's image of me?" But I had already outgrown the label on that box.

Just before this occasion I had a dream of "a crazy woman painting in the kitchen while the lions, tigers and bears look on." Perhaps it was time to dust off more than just my paints and brushes. Let my son meet the larger woman, his Creatrix. Once ignited, could I keep the fire fueled?

Children live out the creative process. They create, manifest, and destroy. And they do it over and over again. Repetition is how they gain mastery and a measure of control over their abilities. The creative process teaches them firsthand that life is not permanent. Change always happens. This is natural. To feel safe in the real world, where everyone is different and things can change at any moment, we need to support their trust in their innate wisdom. The best way to do this is by modeling it ourselves. Rather than delude them with false expectations that we live in a just and orderly world, we can prepare them to face the chaos by nurturing their inner knowing. If our children can learn to trust themselves and their connectedness to all things, they will do the best they can because they are in tune with themselves.

This is a two-way street. The way of the child can help us tune into the wonder of daily adventures and explorations. Tired, cynical adults have forgotten how to play. My son helped me become reenchanted with life in our world. Remembering awe and our connections with all things, also reminded me we are not alone. Many visible and invisible supports are all around us, ready to help if we call them and open to their touch. Reawakening and reopening our inner channels of knowing, and feeding our deepest desires will make us happier to wake every morning, and more eager to participate in whatever each day will bring.

CHAPTER 13
Connecting with Rubybear

A few years after Aaron was born, I started having dreams of losing my wallet and all the identification within it. I even left my handbag, wallet included, in a few shopping carts. I needed some answers about why this was happening so the issues could be addressed. Perhaps it was about losing my old identity. But what would replace it? When I settled down to meditate about all of this, on my forty-fifth birthday, I also requested some serious guidance about the second half of my life.

After a few moments, I started hearing the words, *"Rubybear, Rubybear."* But I was alone. No one spoke those words. Where were they coming from? Who was calling me Rubybear?

Within a year after this experience, two different shamans told me my totem, also known as a power animal, was the Bear.

I recalled my first feelings about bear energy. While pregnant with Aaron, I was in an authentic movement class, feeling vulnerable and facing the fear of losing yet another pregnancy. From deep within a ferocious mama bear energy began to emerge. At one point I became furious about something and growled out loud. Later, people in the building came to see "the bear" in our movement class. I had found my maternal bear! Or she had found me. So my initial association with *Rubybear* was about that maternal energy.

The Native American belief about totem animals is that you are born each lifetime with the same power animal and share similar qualities and characteristics with others who have the same totem animal. Although other animal energies can support you over a lifetime, your totem animal is your main guide. So now I understood that I was a member of the Bear clan. Bear energy is often equated with the maternal. Children are given stuffed bears at birth for protective comfort.

Mother bears are noted for their ferociousness in protecting their young. No one gets in between a female bear and her cubs! I had an abnormal fear of bears when I would travel into wilderness areas where bears roamed. Bears have also crossed my path in some of those regions. My fear of bears subsided a bit when I was pregnant with Aaron. Often when one is extremely attracted to or fearful of an animal, it is because that animal is their power animal.

As Jamie Sams and David Carson point out in their book, the strength of Bear medicine is the power of introspection.[15] In winter, Bear enters the womb-cave to hibernate and digest the year's experiences. In the safety of the womb-cave, Bear attunes to the energies of Mother Earth and receives nourishment from the Great Void, "the place where all solutions and answers live in harmony with the questions that fill our realities." The power of Bear lies in this space of inner knowing, often called the Dream Lodge by native tribes. This is also a place of female receptive energy that allows visionaries, mystics and shamans to prophesize. So Bear is a dream animal, guided by its right brain and intuition to find answers or the sweetness of truth. It is also associated with the Roman goddess Diana, goddess of the moon and the hunt; equivalent to the Greek goddess, Artemis. Interestingly, I had felt most akin to Artemis when I read goddess mythology in earlier years.

Besides animal spirit guides, there are human spirit guides as well. In my studies with Ohky Semine Forest, a Mayan shaman and medicine healer, I learned that we each have a "council of chiefs" or group of guides (five or six) who help us on our earth journey.[16] I often meditate with this group and ask for guidance. At different points in my life, a member of this council revealed themselves to me in a dream or journey and I paid attention to the message that was given. The messages were useful in supporting challenges in my life or a decision that needed to be made.

But there was more to discover about this part of my identity as the years carried me onward. In 1993, while Aaron was still a preschooler, I attended a drum-making workshop. Making my own frame drum was a profound experience. That instrument contains my energy. It is an extension of me, and because of this connection, I rarely let anyone use my drum. Many feel a strong attraction to drums because their sounds and rhythms resemble our mother's heartbeat in utero. By drumming, I felt a deeper connection with the drumbeat of the heart of the earth. And the steady pattern of shamanic drumming took me to deeper levels of meditation.

The percussive instrument that shamans or shamanic practitioners typically use is a frame drum, which has a single drumhead from animal skin or man-made materials and a width greater than its depth. The frame drum has shown up again and again over thousands of years and across continents which is why it is usually the choice for shamanic practitioners. Its role has served in seasonal rituals, community celebrations, rites of passage, initiations, full moon gatherings, and healings as it transforms consciousness into trance-like spacious awareness.

Shamans are typically spiritual healers in indigenous cultures who, with the help of a percussive instrument, journey outside of time and space into non-ordinary reality. In these journeys or trance-like states, shamans retrieve information from helping spirits to aid individuals or their community. David Abram defines a shaman as having "the ability to readily slip out of the perceptual boundaries that demarcate his or her particular culture, the boundaries reinforced by social customs, taboos, and most importantly, the common speech or language in order to make contact with, and learn from, the other powers in the land."[17] This person serves as an intermediary between human and nonhuman worlds. Shamanism goes back over 25,000 years, but in Western cultures today people have trained to become shamanic practitioners using these techniques to help themselves and others bring their lives back into a place of harmony and balance.

Around the time I made my drum, I bought an eighteen-foot-diameter tipi cover and enough lodgepole pine from the Midwest and had like-minded friends help me assemble it. We began drum circles in the tipi. A few years later, when Aaron was in kindergarten at the school next door, the teachers walked their students over for an experience in the tipi. In those sessions, I drummed for them, read Native American stories, and gave out hand instruments like rattles so they could join me in music making. Everyone enjoyed and appreciated the activities.

The gemstone ruby is often seen as a stone of Divine creativity. It boosts energy levels and promotes high self-esteem, intuition and spiritual wisdom. For some it represents love, passion, power and courage. It seems that by receiving the name *Rubybear* I was now on a journey to discover the sweetness of my own heart-truth.

So besides birthing and raising Aaron in mid-life, I was also birthing the essence of *Rubybear* through my spiritual practices of sitting in drumming meditation with my council of chiefs and journeying with my totem animal, Bear. Since shamanism came to me naturally, it was easier to embrace and practice than other spiritual disciplines; the drumming, trance states and empowering communication with animal and spirit helpers, help guide me and others who seek my counsel. I also believe these practices helped me be a better mother, certainly a more present and attentive one. Through our active engagement with each other and experiences through Aaron's childhood and adolescence, we would each grow and stretch ourselves as human beings and expand our capacity to love.

CHAPTER 14
Generational Dreams

felt the pain deep inside as tears came to my eyes. They are playing "The Star Spangled Banner" on opening day of Little League in which my son, Aaron, is now participating. He is six and I am forty-six years old, yet the pain I feel now on hearing this familiar song is the same pain I felt hearing it as a child.

Then I would cry because I was a girl which kept me from fulfilling my father's dream of playing baseball in the major leagues. Sometime, much later on, I resolved my feelings about being born female, which had become even more sour by the time I reached adulthood. But in the here and now, there is still the pain of my father's unfulfilled dream.

In high school my father, Ed, was a tremendous athlete with such promise. It was quoted in one of the many newspaper articles on Ed that he was "a baseball, basketball, and soccer performer of exceptional brilliance." He was being scouted out by major league teams such as the Boston Red Sox to be a pitcher. The St. Louis Cardinals had actually set up a training date for him soon after high school graduation. However, loyalty to his country, eagerness to be involved in the war effort and invincible youthful spirit prompted him to enlist in the Merchant Marines for WWII immediately upon graduation in June of 1943.

After having lost over 40 pounds on his first transatlantic crossing, Ed realized that he didn't have the stomach for sea and transferred to the Army in March, 1944. While in training, he played baseball and could have continued entertaining the troops with his "good whip and keen batting eye," but he chose to go overseas where the action was. His main involvement in the war effort was building bridges and removing land mines. His last post was in Saarbrucken, Germany, where he was a corporal and squad leader. On May 29, 1945, Ed's life changed forever as he stepped unknowingly on a German land mine in France. The consequence of that horrible event was that he lost his left leg, which had to be amputated below the knee, and his right leg was severely damaged.

After waking in a field hospital in Germany, Ed had the profound realization that, with the loss of his leg, he would never play major league ball. The Purple Heart would now replace any baseball trophies he might have won. He told me that he felt severe disappointment for his mother who would not only feel the loss of her son's wholeness but also the loss of a life made easier with the income earned through a professional sports career.

After several surgeries at Walter Reed Hospital requiring a stay of many months, Ed was fitted with a wooden leg. Before he left the hospital he managed to entertain the other patients with his prowess on a basketball court. Even with one leg, Ed managed to pitch for the semi-pro leagues and the University of Connecticut. He earned the reputation of "the fastest ball on the team," not without some distress, however, since he managed to break his wooden leg on the mound several times.

Once Ed had sons, baseball ambition reignited as he dreamed of them fulfilling what he had not. But as talented as my brothers were in sports, they were not major league material. Wrestling with his disappointment, Ed moved on to a spectator sports position with the television which gave him free reign to work out his frustrations at a distance. The rest of us learned that Sunday afternoons were not the time for a laid-back family visit.

So now I stand here with my son, the only male grandchild in the family thus far, wondering if he will fulfill the family dream of major league baseball. Or maybe the dream just doesn't matter so much anymore. But maybe it does. Maybe the deep pain I hold inside for my father's greatest wish from youth denied will lessen if I could hold onto a dream, if someday…

CHAPTER 15
Soccer Mom

I did not sign on for this identity in the beginning. In fact, it was only when Aaron got to high school that I referred to myself as one even though my son played soccer for ten years. I guess when he became a serious player, I became one too. Again, you have to believe me when I say that I did not choose a soccer life. It just happened.

You have all heard about soccer moms and the sacrifices we make daily all year round to drive malodorous vans full of kids around the state, and then the nation, packing them up, washing their grimy, smelly clothing, being faithful fans and cheering for them in all types of weather from near blizzard conditions to desert-scorched fields to knee-high mud puddles to the tune that the game must go on! Bearing ice packs, ankle braces, water and Gatorade, Gatorade, Gatorade (how much can they drink?) to the cry of who got injured in this game and how serious it is and will they be ready for the next game. And, as if one's time is not enough of an expense, there is the financing of it all with high-fashion cleats (I never knew boys could talk about such details!), premier club memberships, and destination costs of air or gasoline travel, hotels and meals. It cost $7,000 one year when my son played on three teams. Soccer adventures became vacation destinations for most families. What a life…many asked me back then what I was going to do when my son stopped playing soccer as if I'd be herded to pasture for early retirement. I really didn't know what would fill that void.

What I want to talk about is the mystery of soccer for me, and perhaps for others, as another aspect of self is revealed. I have always thought of myself as a fairly intelligent, sensitive, tolerant, reasonable, compassionate human being until a soccer game gets heated up. Then some part of me comes alive and it's not always predictable. I have witnessed myself yelling at refs for bad calls, other parents for their nasty behavior and even quarreling with my husband if I feel he's making an unfair assessment of my son's playing. I am ready to go to war…just provoke me! I can't say I'm proud of this behavior and I have tried to control myself, but then it doesn't seem like I'm part of the game. If I distance myself emotionally, I might as well not be there. I used to laugh at "silent sidelines" (maybe it helps the young players). Soccer is an emotional game. At least that's how it is worldwide, and soccer began outside the United States. So why not let it rip…verbally that is, not with physical violence as is the case in other countries.

I am embarrassed thinking back to when, on occasion, I would catch myself running out on the field. Then I'd understand the principle of enmeshment as I found it hard to separate my legs from my son's. The same muscles in my legs started twitching as my son raced to kick the ball. I prayed no one was watching at those times. I have found ways to stop that behavior like forcing myself to sit down or stand behind my digital camera and tripod.

What I hadn't resolved is the emotional funk I would get into after a game that didn't go so well. It was funny to me that my son seemed to get beyond disappointment easier and sooner than I did. Maybe it was because he actually played the game, and my involvement was only from the sidelines and I needed some way to discharge built-up tension. Or as a mom we take on our child's disappointment? I'm not sure. All I know is that the emotional cost of energy was as significant as the physical cost of time and money discussed above. This is starting to sound like one big drain, but I wouldn't trade it for anything. There are rewards; the biggest is sharing something so significant to your child and belonging to a group of others who feel your pain and your joy. So where would I find a substitute for a soccer life when I retired…or, rather, my son retired?

( ))

CHAPTER 16
Initiation

For three consecutive summers (1997-99), my friend and work partner, Wendy, and I led women's retreats in Taos, New Mexico. The theme of these retreats was *Exploring Sacred Spaces* for one's own nourishment. There were mostly experiential activities and rituals: hiking to sacred waterfalls in the mountains and hot springs in the Rio Grande; collecting sage and making prayer bundles; art projects; drumming; writing; and sharing what was discovered during these experiences. Wendy and I enjoyed leading these retreats just as much as the women who participated.

When we did not get enough registrations for the fourth summer and had to cancel the retreat, we were both disappointed. But I understand why it was not meant to be. The universe helped manifest my own pilgrimage to the Southwest so that I could enter the next phase of my life.

Months before, I had seen an advertisement announcing the annual Mescalero Apache Ceremonial Dances and felt frustrated that I would not be able to attend since I would be busy leading our workshop. Well, as fate would have it, our retreat was canceled so now I was free to go to the Apache dances and revisit Chaco Canyon. I had wanted to return to Chaco since the miraculous conception and subsequent birth of Aaron nine years earlier. So I now had a trip for Wendy and me.

I arrived in Albuquerque in June of 2000 and met Wendy and her husband, George. They took me to a store that had an incredible collection of animal fetishes. We spent some time admiring what was there. At some point, I felt a certain rattlesnake fetish call to me. I do not collect fetishes, but there was something about this rattlesnake that wouldn't let me leave it alone. It was primitive-looking, coiled, so that as I looked down on it, it took on the shape of a question mark. The coloring was varied shades of terracotta-earthen tones. It was really quite "striking," so I bought it.

Two days later, Wendy and I arrived for our camping trip in Chaco Canyon. We set up camp and the next day explored the park. It was hot! 108 degrees or so, which was probably the reason why we saw few tourists. I was drawn to visit the great kiva structure at Casa Rinconada. Kivas are circular chambers built wholly or partly underground, traditionally used by male members of the Pueblo people for spiritual ceremonies. After my initial trip to Chaco in 1990, I had read that Chaco Canyon was one of those power spots on the earth's energy grid with its main energy vortex at Casa Rinconada. It was the focal point for all the ceremonial activity in the canyon during the 1987 Harmonic Convergence, the world's first synchronized global peace meditation. This event also closely coincided with an exceptional alignment of planets in the solar system.

The Great Kiva at Casa Rinconada extends sixty-three feet in diameter and is aligned to true north, with a deep womb-like interior. It was built in the 1100s and may have been designed to serve as a core structure for the Chacoan spiritual power matrix. After my visit to this Great Kiva, I read that this was the place where initiates were taken once they served in special ways in their individual pueblos. These chosen ones would convene and bring the energy and the light together so that it could travel out from the great kiva to the great houses and dwellings far away.

As soon as I left the car in the parking lot of the Great Kiva, I could feel the downward pull of energy through my legs as if it were drawing me to the Kiva. With every step toward the Kiva, the energy pull became greater. Once I reached the gate, I was stunned to see it boarded with a

Do Not Enter sign. *This couldn't be*, I thought, because I knew I had to go inside. So, ignoring the sign, I climbed over the rail and down into the belly of the kiva. I walked around a bit admiring the fine masonry of the construction, but the energy had now become strong and had entered my womb, so I decided to take a seat in the shade on the stone ledge attached to the circular perimeter. I started to breathe more deeply, taking in the energy of this sacred place.

I asked for permission to be there, and a chuckled response replied, "Of course, your energy vibration is welcome here." I could feel my heart chakra open, and I experienced the gentleness of other spirits here as well as the gentleness of my own being. The chakras are energy centers along the central meridian in the body. There are seven main ones that are wheels of spinning energy, each corresponding to certain nerve bundles and major organs that move the energy throughout the body. An image came before me of each living being having its own vortex of energy, spiraling between heaven and earth, overlapping with each other. Our energetic connection with all of life became clear. I sat for about a half hour enjoying this energy connection, until I felt it was time to take my leave. Before I left, I asked the energies about my spirit work and whether New Mexico would be a more suitable environment for it. They answered, "While you learn and feel nourished in the Southwest, you are to be the messenger for those that want to learn back east."

Before I climbed out of the kiva, I walked over to an opening beneath the wall that went underground to a smaller inner chamber. I had noticed this chamber when I entered the kiva, and for a moment thought about meditating in that dark space so no one would see me, but something had directed me away from it. When I peered into the darkened room, I saw what looked like a stone altar with a rather large rattlesnake skin lying across it. I quickly scrambled out of the kiva with the realization that I had just shared the kiva space with a rattlesnake. Not only did I share its space, but I seemed to have also connected with its spiraling energy. I glanced once more at the Do Not Enter sign and thought maybe this is why people are not supposed to enter the kiva because of physical encounters with rattlesnakes!

As I walked away from the kiva, I noticed my pants were wet. On closer inspection, I found I was bleeding from my vagina. Being menopausal, I was not expecting a menstrual flow, yet bloodletting had occurred. For the rest of the afternoon I rested in a windswept cave above the ruins and wondered, if these rocks could speak, what stories would they tell?

That night I dreamt of a young man pulling my tongue out. Almost Medusa-like he said, "I will speak what you do not want to hear." I tucked this dream away along with my fetish snake, but other dreams and images followed over the next few months. There was the dream of the coiled snake I was trying to distract by throwing something behind it so I would not have to meet it head on. In another dream snakes were biting my fingertips; then in reality, I kept nicking my fingers with knives. Sensations were coming more frequently in my chest and arms, forcing me to make movements connecting my arms with the energy in my chest. I was having visions of painting with both arms, not knowing what needed to be expressed, but knowing something was moving up and needing to get expressed outwards. I decided to consult with a sister guide to help me sort out what was happening.

My visit to Dorothy, a shamanic practitioner, helped give shape, meaning and validation to my experience. With her I journeyed back to the kiva at Chaco Canyon and met the rattlesnake spirit. In my spirit mind, I drew back into the experience of the kiva as much as possible. I became aware of swirling snake energy creating the space of the kiva. The snake moved faster and faster, then stood directly before me and said, "I am your mate, your match." Then the snake entered my vagina, splitting me open, traveling upwards through my body until its tongue flickered through my mouth. "I speak my truth," it said. My body went into rhythmic rocking as the snake traveled through it. There was pain in the intestinal area that felt like my back could break. When I felt fearful during this experience, I received the message "do not worry, you have control of the intensity for what you feel."

After about twenty minutes or so, the journey subsided and I was left with electrified energy internally, as if I had truly "mated" or merged with something. I shared my experience with Dorothy and she told me of her vision while I was journeying. She saw me standing with the snake on one side of the stone slab in the inner chamber of the kiva. My book, this book you are reading, was lying open on the stone slab with a dragon standing on the other side of it saying, "I'm going to dance with you." That was interesting to me since the year before dancing dragon images had come to me and I had even purchased a small replica of one. In addition, this memoir is planned to be published in the Chinese year of the dragon, 2024!

The images in my journey and dreams began making sense. It seems I needed to integrate snake spirit energy into my being to help release the creative energy I hold down in my belly. The rattlesnake, in particular, will help "rattle" and shake free the adhesions in my second chakra area so that my creative energies can be unleashed. The snake goes through transformation every time it sheds its skin. That's what was lying on the stone slab. It's an old life, a former identity given up for a new one.

There have been other times in my life when snakes or dreams of snakes will come to me when I am about to go through a transition of some kind. One remarkable episode happened in 2014. To further my studies in shamanism, I went to Maine for a weekend in June that year to be with Nepalese Shaman Bhola Banstola. In the workshop I learned about Himalayan shamanic practices and techniques to use in my own work. Of special interest was learning about the Nagas, spiritual deities who are half human and half cobra. There were rituals and exercises that we did during the weekend bringing in energy from the Nagas. After I returned home, I practiced what I had learned. Not many days into my practice, a very strange situation developed in my home. Snakes were coming into the master bathroom that connected to my bedroom. I would hear them and wake to see them on the bathroom floor, usually one at a time. They were young snakes, not very big, of garter or black variety. Needless to say, I was freaked out wondering what I was stirring up. My husband had to remove the snakes and take them outdoors since I could not do it. It turned out that the snakes were coming in from the septic through my toilet. The situation was remedied when the septic workers cleaned out the tank. But it is interesting that the snakes, seven in number, came through the toilet in my bathroom when we had three other toilets in the house. I did end my practice of calling in the Nagas after the appearance of snakes in my home!

This book is a creative, spiritual manifestation that I wish to bring into the world. It lies on the stone slab as my offering so that others may be free to express their own creative, spiritual voices. Dancing dragons, serpentine animals, move to fire-breathing creativity. That fire, like the venom of the rattlesnake, contains a poisonous punch, spitting out truth that hurts and heals, destroys and creates. A bittersweet taste lingers on my tongue as I feel the force of what I may say or do that may be painful as well as transforming. The bloodletting from my Chaco Canyon adventure is a sign of the pain, the sacrifice, that must be in breaking new ground, in becoming an initiate in the mystery of metamorphosis. My transformation had begun.

CHAPTER 17
Adonis

I have a son, Aaron, aka Adonis. He truly seemed a gift from the gods…a stunning, virile male at 15 years of age. Even some of the neighborhood moms would watch from their living room windows as Aaron would go running by. I now understand why the Greeks loved young boys. I found such joy bathing in my son's beauty. Oh happy self to gaze upon his light… such pure spirit, mind and body. What pleasure I received watching his athletic form take to martial arts or storm his way down a soccer field. Pride, yes, but more is this mother's embrace of perfection of what I love most, my son. It is he who rises above all else and gives me joy. Yet as all things come to pass, so did the perfect beauty of my son.

A stumble split that divine face tearing flesh that never again will be as before…a glaring mark above the right brow for me to forever see. Now my joy for my once perfect son is accompanied by waves of sadness, then anger, that such unspoiled beauty will no longer be. And I have realized that over these past few months that this scar marks an ending of youth and transition to manhood for it is not just the scar that has changed his face, but his features have altered as well bringing maturity in its wake. So now I see before me the grown-up man who leads a life of imperfection as do I. Hopes for perfection are dashed and replaced with acceptance that life is a path of striving for perfection while reconciling imperfection with each step.

CHAPTER 18
The Light in His Eyes

When Aaron was eight years old, we were told by the long-time psychic I consulted with that he had come into this life "to leave a gift of music." Marvin and I chuckled, thinking that Pam Hogan the psychic, who is usually spot on, was way off base this time, since Aaron showed no inclination toward music. He was also a child who did not like attention in social situations or being center stage. Little did we know that music would soon consume him and become the number one passion in his life. It even replaced soccer toward the end of his high school years.

Unbeknownst to us, Aaron started to make up his own songs around age 16. He would develop the music with some of his friends and even appeared in the talent show for his high school.

That was the first time we heard Aaron sing his own songs. Their performance blew away the audience since each of the boys in the band were known as "the jocks" in the school. Some months later, the boys, then called NOG JAM, performed at Toad's Place, a concert venue and nightclub in New Haven, Connecticut.

It was after that show that I knew what my son was here to do. Pam's pronouncement was indeed true. When I looked into my son's eyes that night I saw the light of his soul. It shone clear and bright and was the essence of who he was. This was when he was happiest: making and performing his music.

There was a time in high school when I wondered if Aaron had attention-deficit hyperactivity disorder. He was a good student, in mostly advanced placement classes earning high grades, but sometimes I would see him tune out and have a faraway look. When I asked Pam about this she told me that Aaron was "hearing music." She told me to ask him what was happening when this occurred, and I did. Aaron's response supported what she had said, and he even thought that this was natural and that everybody heard music. I told him that neither his dad nor I heard music. Perhaps then he realized this was his special gift.

Today, at age 32, Aaron has achieved recognition and success with his music. He has written and produced over 100 songs, including many music videos. Some of them reach prestigious playlists, radio stations and fans around the world. He has toured around this country a few times and started to perform abroad. It is a difficult profession in that the financial support for artists and musicians is nonexistent except for the small percentage who make it "BIG." While this fact gets him down at times, he continues to believe in himself and his music. The creativity keeps coming and he keeps writing and performing songs with other artists. Such a diverse, talented group of musicians he is connected to! A lot of his songs speak of love, relationships and loss; it seems evident that he is the child of psychotherapists. We have supported Aaron's dreams, whether it be soccer or music, and encouraged him to follow his heart's passion and he is doing that. The light in his eyes shines on.

CHAPTER 19
Graduation Letter, 2009

From the belly, in the womb,
Sperm and egg joined bathing in sweet, strong light,
One energy becoming YOU!

Eighteen years in the making of countless hours being with the many
*   aspects of your uniqueness. A mixture of emotion draws me near to*
*   the one strongest pulse of my life, YOU, Aaron Taos.*

I held you in inner space for nine months and then commandeered the
*   outer space of your life.*
I hope I have not been too overBEARing...sometimes, for sure.

I felt a strong responsibility to support your growth in whatever ways
*   possible.*
As a parent, there never seemed to be enough time or years to give so
*   much to one's own.*
Your father would say much the same.

AARON TAOS… you have ripened into the wondrous being that
*   you are bringing joy to us for all of our efforts.*
You may be grateful for us giving you life, but we are far more grateful
*   for the riches you have brought us.*

Go forward my son. May you continue to be blessed in this life with the
Light of your ancestors and the protection of your guardians.
Yes, follow your dreams and your passions with wisdom and discipline.

Keep a true heart, first to yourself, then to others and all of your
*   relations.*
For this you will be at peace with whatever happens in life.
You will forever be in our circle of LOVE and LIGHT.

CHAPTER 20
Shamanic Practice and Painting

n January 2009, five months before Aaron's high school graduation, we bought our first house in New Mexico. It was in the town of Truth or Consequences. Yes, that is a town of about 6,000 people in southern New Mexico, approximately 100 miles north of the Mexican border. The town's original name was Hot Springs, but they changed the name when Ralph Edwards, host of the radio show, "Truth or Consequences," offered in 1950 to broadcast from any city that changed its name to that of the show. So Truth or Consequences, or "T or C" as residents refer to it, was born.

My friend Wendy had moved there with her husband in 1997 and I had visited her there many times, participated in drum circles and met members of the community. We enjoyed the relaxed, communal vibe of the town, and the biggest lake in New Mexico, Elephant Butte, was ten minutes away for Marvin's fishing interests. T or C was known for their 35 artesian wells and springs, which were considered sacred grounds for the Warm Springs Apaches for centuries. The first spiritual guide who revealed himself to me in the early '90s was Cochise, so I felt a kinship with the Apaches and this area.

During one of my visits to the area, a spacious and affordable house was about to go on the market. Aaron was soon to graduate and head off to college. About to become "empty nesters," Marvin and I needed a new focus for our energies. What I liked most about this perfect house was the converted garage space. A previous owner had turned it into a huge painting studio. Marvin and I bought the house, which became our new part time home. This proved to be a good choice.

Although I had already been drumming, journeying and painting for a decade before we purchased the T or C house, once we spent time there, my shamanic practice blossomed since I finally had the time and space to deepen my dedication to my work. During the nine years we owned property there, we enjoyed many happy months in T or C. Those were special times, akin to a "second honeymoon" phase, which brought out the best in each of us and deepened our relationship.

Adjusting to being "empty nesters" can be a difficult transition period. I recommend parents plan early for how they will spend their time once their children have left home. Avoid the despair some parents sink into without a conscious refocusing process to get them through this period. Ideally these efforts may reawaken their marriage relationship while revitalizing individual interests.

In 2010, I began training with Sandra Ingerman, one of the most highly regarded teachers and writers of shamanism today.[18] After the introductory workshop, I attended her Soul Retrieval Training in 2012, followed by Medicine of the Earth in 2015. In Soul Retrieval Training, we were taught how to help others retrieve "lost parts" of their soul essence, to reintegrate their scattered energies and to restore their sense of wholeness. Then I applied to become a shamanic practitioner. After being accepted, my name was listed on Sandra's website. In addition to being a licensed psychotherapist, I was able to combine shamanic techniques and practices in assisting clients who wanted to focus on their spiritual issues.

Around this time, I began co-facilitating a women's shamanic drumming group in Connecticut. We began in October of 2010 and the community has continued to meet monthly, for over thirteen years. I fondly call this circle of women *Sisters of the Drum*. We have been a source of wisdom and support to each other, witnessing spiritual journeys and transformational life events. As a wisdom council, we share the teachings revealed to us from the spirit world during our shamanic journey times together. These teachings have helped us personally and provided guidance and corrective perspectives on world dilemmas, and wiser ways we can use to connect and assist all living beings on our planet.

In the early months of 2011, while visiting our New Mexico home, I was reading about Mary Magdalene in addition to my training with Sandra Ingerman. One day a vision appeared over my left shoulder and despite my attempts to shake it off, it would not leave me. Finally I asked the vision, "What do you want from me?"

"Paint me," it replied.

"I do not paint figures."

Undeterred they responded, "We will help you."

I went out to my studio and painted a 40" by 30" canvas of the figure within three hours. I thought the visions were done, but another one came two days later, with instructions to paint it.

Again, I felt guided to paint this second figure. The second painting was completed in three hours. And on it continued until a total of thirteen paintings, all of the same size, came through. Each was completed within three hours. This process made no sense to me. I had no logical understanding of why this was happening. When I asked my guides in meditation, this is what they shared.

"This group of thirteen paintings, to be titled The Mary Paintings, are aspects of the Divine Feminine that need to be out in the world today. The Divine Feminine is revealing herself more and more at this time to support the evolution of consciousness and the energetic alignment of the planet so that men and women can develop to their highest potential for the greater good and live in universal harmony, peace and love."

I was told this collection of thirteen paintings was not to be broken up or sold, but gifted to an environment that supported the Divine Feminine. The messages for each painting were revealed a year later. At that time I was instructed to make cards of the paintings to sell so they would be out in the world. Each set was to be presented wrapped in a red cloth, inside a prayer-like folder, tied with a gold ribbon and fleur de lis. I listened and carefully followed the exact instructions. In 2015, I was asked by the Sisters of Mercy nuns to exhibit these paintings at their retreat and conference center, Mercy by the Sea, in Madison, Connecticut. The paintings are still there and will remain so indefinitely.

I have sold over 800 sets of the cards and have received many favorable comments over the years. People have used the cards in women's groups, as writing prompts in workshops and in personal meditations. If I had not listened to the voices/my inner guides, the meaning and richness of what the paintings represent would not be out in the world today. How many times do we ignore those voices trying to communicate messages and clues daily? Taking the time to listen and pay attention to them can have meaningful impacts on our personal lives, as I've learned over and over, and quietly make our world a better place.

In conjunction with The Mary Paintings exhibit, I started offering shamanic painting workshops, initially at the same venue, Mercy by the Sea. By combining my love of painting, shamanism, and group process, others could learn to access their own guidance without intermediaries. Facilitating these workshops has brought me as much joy as the participants who discover their own messages via the painting process.

So many spiritual practices have guided and supported my life. In hindsight I can see how essential they have been so I share the details despite knowing some readers may find my experiences implausible when comparing them to their own. But my pregnancy losses compelled me to seek other ways, and especially when caring for my husband during his years of failing health; these ways once again preserved my sanity. To remain present, spiritually as well as physically, mentally and emotionally, during Marvin's demise would not have been possible without these prior preparations. They allowed us to experience the healing which resolved our karmic past.

CHAPTER 21
The Transitional Deaths of Parents

Just as pregnancy losses and births can be full of karmic resolutions, so can the final passages of parents and loved ones. As mentioned earlier, I believe our children choose the parents they want to be incarnated with in any particular lifetime. As my parents had aged, and my spiritual awakenings continued, I began to wonder about why I'd chosen mine and whether our lessons were being completed.

I probably picked my father because he was strong and confident, a wise man who lived as he saw fit. Ed got things done. He lived as if he had two legs to stand on instead of one. Even though I was born female, I modeled myself mostly after my father, since I saw him as the more powerful and appealing role model. My mother, on the other hand, taught me how *not* to be in the world. Arline, however, did teach me about the importance of communication and compassion. Both were important teachings in shaping who I have become… a strong, confident, compassionate woman who is an effective communicator and manifester of dreams and ideas. Of course there were many other attributes, good and bad, that I learned from each parent.

Ed had several close calls with death. It is not an exaggeration to say I had been preparing for my father's death since age twelve, when his gallbladder almost exploded, with a stone the size of a grapefruit. I probably wrote about a half a dozen eulogies for my father at these "close call" times, but none of them was ever read. My mother had always said that my father would bury her first and she was right!

I never wrote a eulogy for my mother until after her death. Hers came so quickly and I was not prepared. *Mothers don't die. They are eternal, aren't they?* My siblings were not prepared either. We all thought my dad would predecease her and she would grow old in peace finally getting the solitude and freedom from caring for others that she so desired and deserved. Things worked out differently. I guess mom went to Plan B, her dying first, when she realized my father was too stubborn to leave.

Before she was diagnosed with cancer, my mother expressed her usual symptoms of being tired all the time and lacking energy. We all thought it was her age or the previous year's diagnosis of atrial fibrillation acting up in combination with being worn out from not getting "the retirement" from my father that she thought she deserved. "Men retire from the workplace. Why couldn't I retire from my duties at home?" Arline would quip. We, her children, would offer suggestions and opportunities to change her life, but her Catholic guilt and sense of responsibility would kick in preventing her from altering her life path.

When my mother mentioned going to her internist for the nth time, I told her that I wanted to go with her and ask him some questions to help diagnose what could be going on with her. I didn't usually go with my mother to her doctor appointments, but something inside ordered me to go. My mother reluctantly agreed knowing I had to drive an hour to pick her up for the appointment. In the meeting, I asked the doctor to do a chest x-ray. He agreed and sent us next door. I remember my mother sliding down in her chair, almost to the floor from fatigue as we waited for the results. Just two weeks before, I had taken her to shop for a coat at L.L. Bean and she was charging ahead of me in the store while I had difficulty keeping up with her. Now she couldn't even sit upright in her chair. *What was up with that?* After what seemed like hours, someone told us to return to the internist's office so he could speak to us about the results.

"Ominous" was the word the doctor used when he told us my mother had tumors in her lungs, probably cancerous. He felt her abdomen and said there was swelling around her lymph nodes and he ordered a CT scan for the next day. We left the office stunned, slowly trying to comprehend the news. There was a prescription for my dad to pick up at a nearby pharmacy. As we waited, we discussed the possibility of my mother having "the big C," as she put it. She immediately took the blame for it saying it was due to her smoking, even though she always told us she never inhaled, and gave up smoking over ten years before. I told her I was sorry this was happening to her. She had had a hard life and now she had to contend with this. We were both still in shock and had trouble finding our emotions.

When we returned home, she went to prepare dinner and I went into the den to tell my father where things stood. My mother came into the room while I was talking, probably to validate what she had heard earlier. My father expressed his sorrow to my mother. There was a brief emotional interaction as we agreed to wait for all the test results before committing ourselves to accept the situation as terminal.

As we stood together, I remembered the evening at my parents' home two weeks before, after the coat shopping expedition, when I stayed late. Each of them had been flat out in their respective recliners with me lying on the couch, watching TV. This was a rarity. An odd scenario, just the three of us, the initial triangle of our family, reassembled once more. Usually one of my siblings would be around, rarely us three. Looking back, it felt like an ending of sorts, one last gathering of the initial fold. I left my parents to their own thoughts saying I would call in the morning.

I never called that morning. My father called me first to say my mother was taken by ambulance to the hospital because she couldn't breathe. Arline never returned home again. She died six weeks later. My mother could have returned home to die, but she chose not to. Arline finally left my father after fifty-seven years of marriage. She didn't want to share the same space with him ever again. We siblings assured her we would find some arrangement for our father if she wanted to return home, but she refused, saying he had a right to be there with all of his ailments. It would also be hard to see hired help caring for Ed in ways she no longer could, and not have them do things "the right way," her way. Even after my mother died, my father made his caretakers keep the house exactly as my mother kept it, even though it didn't make sense at times. Whether Arline wanted distance from Ed, or wanted to avoid feeling useless since she could no longer fulfill her mission in life, we do not know for sure, but she refused to return home. I think it was a little of both.

In the hospital, my mother received a prognosis of three to six months with the possibility of prolonging her life if she had chemotherapy, which she refused. Once my mother got the news, she was ready to go sooner, rather than later. I helped prepare her for death by doing loving meditations and visualizations, anointing her with lavender oil, releasing the negativity of this lifetime, forgiving and opening to the Light of the beyond. We spoke of our triangulated relationship with my father and wished it were different. I needed to hear her say I was "her daughter" since she frequently said I was my "father's daughter." In the end, she owned me.

In those six weeks, we discussed many topics. Toward the end, she could not speak as the tumors pressed against her voice box. I could feel her withdrawing, into herself, and another world. During our last meditation together, I could no longer feel her presence. Afterward, I sat beside her on the bed. She opened her eyes briefly, not quite grasping what they were seeing. With tears streaming down my face, I told her for the last time I loved her and would miss her. Mustering what strength she had left, my mother slowly lifted her unsteady hand to my cheek and caressed it silently. Her hand spoke what her voice could not: a loving, gentle farewell.

A day later, when Arline died, she did it quietly and gently, slipping into the night without fanfare or fuss. She did it in her own time and in her own way. My siblings and I were with her for her last breath. I miss my mother. I wish we could have played more together. We did share some deep belly laughs, over the silliest things no one else in the room would understand. Were we close? Yes, in some ways, no in other ways. We did not talk every day. Weeks would go by between visits. But deep invisible threads connected us. When she gave birth to my siblings, even though I was miles away, unaware her labor had begun, my body registered the pangs of labor. After the fateful visit to her internist, I felt once again "in labor," my womb-like connection with my mother undeniable. Sensing our earthly ties had to be cut, I needed to let go, to let her return to the Great Unknown.

CHAPTER 21

When I sit holding an old scarf of my mom's, I sometimes feel her energy, the hollowness of regret, a life not well lived, not explored in ways I feel life should be lived. I remember hugging her…hugging her hollowness as if nothing of substance was there. It was hard for her to hug back. Nothing remained to give. The weight of the years of service to others snuffed out her energy. My mother wanted a better life for me. That wish has been granted. I say, "Rest in peace, mom, your caretaking days are over. May your next life be a celebration of joy, for you deserve so much better." Arline died on Wednesday, November 14, 2007, under the crescent sliver of a waxing new moon. It seems she was a young soul and had much to learn of earthly existence through further reincarnations.

In contrast, and possibly in a symbolic representation of why my parents had a conflicted relationship, my father died under the very last stage of a waning crescent, before a new moon. He was most likely an old soul, having lived many lives on this earth, while my mother was just getting started. Ed died at age eighty-nine on January 19, 2015, under what is called a balsamic moon, just before the new moon on January 20. This may have been his last life on earth, no longer needing to reincarnate, to resolve any more karma. Maybe that is why he lingered the last ten years, with neuropathic pain and other ailments, to make sure everything was accounted for so there would be no coming back. I am at peace, knowing he has moved on to the next plane, where I also hope to be when my life ends a final time. He was determined to have a successful outcome on this go-around. "Well, you did it, Dad! I am so proud of you and your efforts that have earned your success. Your travels on the earth have come to a close. I bid you farewell."

My siblings, our spouses and all the children gathered at our family home to be with my father as he made his transition. The hospice nurse was called in to administer medication. My son, Aaron, had just returned to the U.S. from a trip to Argentina only hours before. Ed seemed to have waited until we were all present for him to take his last breath. We did not have to wait long before he expired.

I felt immediately swept up into a vortex of energy with my father as he traveled through this portal. He looked back at me and said, "Hey, this ain't so bad!" Then he continued drifting upwards with his body whole, both legs now intact. I was mesmerized, feeling every cell in my body electrified, as I experienced this union with the Divine. When it was over, it took me a few moments to return to the room where everyone else was grieving. I was elated but did not feel it was right to share what had happened with me while the others were struggling with their emotions. But for years afterwards, I savored that beautiful experience. It lessened my grief since I felt for certain my father was in a better place.

Ed was the hero of my youth…the warrior I modeled myself after. "You are strong like your father," my mother would say. She distanced herself from me knowing my father's pull was magnetic. I was his daughter. So the story unfolded. Not until early adulthood did I cast the other eye to notice what I owed to my mother, as she had formed me as well. When embracing feminism in my early twenties, my mother and I became closer. We would talk on the phone for hours. My father and I spoke less as the years went by. He seemed to accept that my mother and I needed to have more of a relationship. When I would call and he answered the phone, it was a quick hello and then he would yell to my mother, "Cathy's on the phone." Then mutter a quick goodbye and hang up.

After my mother's death, my relationship with my father became closer. I was glad to have seven more years with him. We would talk, go visit his doctors, enjoy ice cream jaunts, and drive to the cemetery to visit my mother's grave. After she died, whenever my father would go through a rough patch, I would encourage him to reminisce about happier times, when he was a child, or in the early years of my parents' marriage. Ed would smile and share a few memories, but invariably he would recall what I was like as a baby or young child. The stories would be about taking me to UCONN to meet his baseball coach from college or bringing me to his job so his colleagues could play with me. There was such pride and joy on his face from recounting those experiences. It was in those moments that I knew I was truly loved.

My parents were an integral part of my journey on this earth. Their love and influence, both positive and negative, was consciously and unconsciously contained within me. Whether I was far away, or within reach, my appreciation of the parts they played grew as with my developing awareness. My choice of a career, to dedicate my life's work to understanding relational conflicts and the many ways love is expressed, was hardly by accident. Even the choice of my partner, Marvin, was in keeping with my parents' respect for hard work, education, ambition, loyalty and caring. As an adolescent my father told me to "marry someone Jewish because they take good care of their wives"!

Lastly, being present and involved with each of my parent's respective transitions to death helped prepare me for the next loss, and what was to come with my husband.

CHAPTER 22
From Love, Not Obligation

Marvin could have left this Earth many times during his life. There were many hospital visits for various ailments over our years together. He endured many bodily repairs, and even invasive hardware, so he could be with Aaron and me for as long as possible. We are grateful he stayed as long as he did. Our 1983 honeymoon was a portent of the relationship Marvin and I would have with illnesses over our 38 years together. During the second week of our trip to Greece he was ill with abdominal pain and nausea. He had taken the antibiotic doxycycline, as a preventative for stomach bacteria, and it ulcerated his esophagus. Once diagnosed and treated, he regained his health enough to enjoy our third and last week in Greece.

Almost ten years later, Marvin had a brush with death in the spring of 1992. Our family took a trip to Paradise Island in the Bahamas. While I was playing with ten-month-old Aaron on the beach, Marvin went snorkeling. He had an angina attack, which immobilized every muscle except his toes. Luckily Marvin was wearing flippers, and he very slowly made his way back to shore. All the while he was watching us on the beach, hoping he would make it back to be with us again. Once back on land, he regained use of his muscles, but he knew something was seriously wrong. Many times Marvin would recall this frightening event. It was our reminder of how precious life is, and that he was almost deprived of the chance to see our son, Aaron, grow up.

Upon our return to Connecticut, Marvin went through a cardiac assessment. It revealed four blockages in his arteries. He needed open heart surgery for the 99% blockage of his LAD (left anterior descending artery), often called "the widow-maker" artery. The operation was scheduled for the day before Aaron's first birthday. It was a challenging time for us. I worried about complications or consequences from the surgery, while supporting Marvin, and managing our one-year-old, along with fielding calls from clients at our respective places of employment. Fortunately the surgery was successful, and we made it through this difficult time. One thing that helped me settle down before bed during these long, trying days of Marvin's hospitalization was a beer and a cigarette out on the porch at night. I am not advocating for either, but sometimes returning to old habits, briefly, can be comforting.

For the next twenty-five years, Marvin's health was relatively stable. He had a few emergency room visits, and brief hospital stays for blood pressure issues and irregular heart rhythms. Eventually he had a pacemaker inserted into his chest. In May of 2017 his health issues started to intensify. At the beginning of that month an astrologer told me from 2017 to 2021, "Your life will revolve around sickness and health issues, mostly caring for those around you." She apologized for the information in that reading since it foretold a prolonged period of troubling times around illness, but she also said there would be "surprises" along the way. "You need to be present and focused, and own your own intuition." Around the same time another healer told me I needed to accept "disruption" in my life, and the sooner I accepted this new way of learning, the gentler it would be.

None of this made me happy, but it did give me some perspective on where my life was headed in the short term. After the astrological reading during our trip to New Mexico in May of 2017, Marvin had to be hospitalized in Albuquerque for congestive heart failure. When he was released after a few days, we returned to Connecticut. For the most part, Marvin re-stabilized. But later that year, he started to receive spinal injections for his severe back issues.

Because of Marvin's declining health, and Wendy moving away from New Mexico the previous year, we decided to sell our home in T or C in late 2017. Our agreement was that I still needed a place in New Mexico if we were to sell in T or C, so we made a plan to look at properties in Taos where there were more stimulating activities and where I would feel comfortable being alone if his health interfered with his joining me. Taos had always been a special place for me since the time I interned with Ted Egri, the sculptor, in the '80s and led women's retreats in the '90s.

I had always felt an important parallel connection with Bolivia when I visited Taos. No wonder I felt at home in Taos, with its Native American and Hispanic populations. The people and the place echo with a cultural richness comparable to Bolivia, which so deeply imprinted me in my twenties. The Taos Pueblo is the only living Native American community designated as a National Historic Landmark and a UNESCO World Heritage Site. This New Mexican settlement, north-northeast of Santa Fe, has managed to retain a thriving traditional community of Pueblo Indians. They've borrowed from the Anglo and Spanish invader cultures without losing their distinctive cultural integrity despite centuries of contact.

Just as mountains surround La Paz, the city of Taos is nestled between mountains of the Sangre de Cristo range — 7,000 feet above sea level. Along the outskirts of Taos, small villages like Arroyo Seco reminded me of the communities encircling La Paz. Just as La Paz once nurtured and supported me, in Taos I feel the same creative and spiritual energies of the Divine Feminine. Once again, I feel my heart open in ways that it had while living in Bolivia. Taos feels like a motherland to me. As La Paz taught me to just "be" and relax into myself, Taos inspires the same sense of comfort and security. My Connecticut home base feels more like the fatherland. There I am more proactive, caught up in the whirl of doing and taking care of necessities.

In early 2018, Marvin was told he needed a left hip replacement so plans to look for a house in Taos were delayed. It took many weeks to see if he could be cleared for surgery because of his heart issues. He ended up having the surgery in May. Even though the surgery went well, his blood pressure was unstable so it took longer for him to recover in the hospital. He also needed to go to a rehab facility for a couple of weeks to gain enough strength to return home. When Marvin did come home, he needed the Visiting Nurses Association and physical therapy for several more weeks, but it was mostly me who did the caretaking. I was scheduled to go on a writer's retreat in New Mexico, but had to cancel because of Marvin's condition.

This new role of prolonged caretaking was unsettling. The understanding in our household was that I would get to be my own priority when Marvin retired. His career as a clinical psychologist and pioneer in the responsible gambling field was quite demanding. (Marvin received many rewards for his career efforts, most notably the Lifetime Achievement Award.) So I became the central figure on the home front, managing household responsibilities, finances, rental properties and decisions on raising Aaron, while working and trying to have creative time. The plan that my life would become my own did not work out very well since there were only a few years between the time Marvin retired at 75, and his health started to decline.

Marvin did feel badly about this and would often emphasize that he was ready to support both Aaron's needs and mine, and our creative passions anyway he could: "I told you, and I'm showing you that it's your turn with all my support and love. I am so sorry my failing health interferes with what you need to do for yourself. Please take care of yourself every day. I deeply appreciate the love and caring you give to me. But you are most important, and I will try to help you live life the way you deserve. I'll always love and appreciate who you are, whatever happens."

Marvin's words were a turning point for me in my attitude about caregiving. Earlier, during his hip replacement recovery at home, there was an incident where he set the microwave on too long. What was in it caught fire. This happened the first time I left him alone to go exercise. Upon my return home, I found firetrucks and medical personnel attending Marvin. Because of pain medication, he did not remember turning the microwave on. He had panicked with the smoke in the house, and ran upstairs to find the source of it, reinjuring his hip.

I was beside myself! Now I could not even exercise? I hit bottom, feeling my life was being squeezed out of me, and that there was no freedom to care for my own needs. Obligation to care for Marvin's needs was all there was room for. I became angry and resentful. After this episode, Marvin wrote the words above, and I understood he would love me unconditionally, even with my caretaking limitations. This is when my caring for him started to come from love rather than obligation. I guess this was one of the "surprises" the astrologer spoke of.

After Marvin's full recovery from hip surgery, he became independent again. But his health was precarious. Knowing this, I was learning about "disruption." I truly accepted the role of being his caregiver for the foreseeable future. Developing this belief of acceptance helped me evolve. My energy started to come from a place of love instead of mere marital obligation. This shift changed our dynamics. It helped me attend to my husband's debilitating health needs over the next few years.

CHAPTER 23
All Things Must Pass

n February 2019, Marvin had to be hospitalized in Naples, Florida, for congestive heart failure. After a few days he was released, but he never adequately recovered. When we saw his cardiologist after returning home, the doctor referred Marvin for an evaluation with Yale's Center for Advanced Heart Failure. That evaluation was a game-changer. It revealed, in addition to cardiac and kidney issues, that Marvin had cardiac amyloidosis. This is a stiffening of the heart muscle, due to protein deposits from the liver going into the heart. The prognosis was not good: maybe a few years to live. However, a drug newly approved by the FDA that May, Vyndaqel, would help stabilize the protein. But it could not cure the disease. The news that this drug could delay Marvin's demise was welcomed, but the fact that the medication cost $18,500 per month, if our insurance did not cover it, was not good news. After three months of rigorous research, and many phone calls, I was able to get our insurance to cover the cost of the medicine. But even with the Vyndaqel, Marvin barely lived two years after his diagnosis.

He had another hospitalization at Yale in August 2019 to remove fluid from around his heart. They surgically inserted a CardioMEMS device in his pulmonary artery to effectively monitor fluid buildup from home. Before that hospitalization, I went to Taos, New Mexico, for a few days to look at houses. Marvin wanted to help with the purchase of a home there before he died, since he wanted me to have some place to go that I loved: "I want to know that I have helped you achieve your wishes. It gives me comfort in knowing that you will have a life after I am gone."

On that trip I found the right house and Marvin helped me finalize the sale in early September. We thought he would be well enough to see it, but sadly he was not able to travel to New Mexico again.

After the August 2019 hospitalization, Marvin's health continued to deteriorate in various ways. This affected my work schedule too so we started planning to hire some help. But first we wanted to take one last trip to Florida. We went in February of 2020 and, although Marvin enjoyed some fishing time with Aaron, he was generally unwell. For the first time he said, "I think I'm dying."

That year, in early May, Marvin tried medical marijuana and Compazine for nausea. He became quite confused and disoriented. We went to the emergency department and after doing some lab work they admitted him to Saint Raphael's Hospital in New Haven, Connecticut. All of this happened in the middle of COVID fears rising, so I was not permitted to be in the hospital with him.

I was beside myself with worry, especially after they put him on the wrong hospital service initially. The hospital staff kept asking me why he was there. Marvin also had some hospital delirium. I would get calls from him saying irrational things like, "I don't know why this reputable doctor is going to do surgery on me down by the lake."

I would reassure him there was no discussion or reason for surgery. Finally, Marvin was put on the correct hospital service and the proper tests were started. Unfortunately, the test results were not good. His low heart pressures indicated advanced heart weakness. He was given six to nine months to live.

We were all devastated by this news. We expected Marvin would live longer, especially with taking Vyndaqel. The only intervention this medical team suggested was Milrinone, a heart medication administered every twenty-four hours through a heart pump. It could give Marvin some energy, but it would not prolong his life. This meant I had to learn how to change out his heart pump daily. What a responsibility! We agreed to this treatment option. A line was surgically inserted to his heart via a port in his chest so he could receive the milrinone. The pump proved to be effective, and Marvin was released from the hospital with palliative care orders. We had to readjust our lives to this new reality. We would not be physically together for much longer. Aaron put his life on hold in Los Angeles and flew home to be with his dad and me in Connecticut for whatever time was left for us to be a family.

Our "love nest" lasted for the next eight months. The three of us savored being together. We shared many precious moments, replaying old family videos, especially of Aaron's growing up years, and celebrating the memories we'd made during the times we were fortunate to have. In the evenings we hung out together, watching nature and music documentaries. We wrote love letters to each other and celebrated our birthdays and our last wedding anniversary. Aaron wrote music and sang his songs of loving and letting go of his dad. I drummed and we meditated together. We laughed and we cried.

During the summer months, Marvin was well enough for Aaron to take him out on Long Island Sound in their boat for some final fishing trips. Over the years father and son had enjoyed many fishing adventures. That shared activity defined their relationship. When Marvin came home from the hospital we hired some excellent help to assist us. These caregivers were a married couple. At first, the man came in the afternoons to be with Marvin to allow me to focus on running errands and taking care of household business.

In September, Marvin fell and broke some ribs. We had to bring in hospice, for pain management, and a hospital bed. After a week, we had to let go of hospice and return to palliative care in order to keep the heart pump. Medicare would not pay for it if Marvin was on hospice care. We also stepped up homecare. The wife of the couple did the day shifts and her husband did the overnight shifts, five days a week. This was so necessary. For me to be awake and present for the challenges and decisions that had to be made daily, I needed to sleep soundly overnight. Aaron and I were with Marvin late afternoons and evenings every day, including weekend days and nights. Sometimes it felt like too much for us. Yet we understood our time with Marvin was limited. And with the risks caused by the COVID pandemic, we did not want to hire anyone else.

On most weekends Marvin looked forward to joining me in our marriage bed for an afternoon nap. Getting him into our bed was a feat but he was so happy when we could make that happen. His eyes would light up whenever I asked if he would like to go to "big mama's bed." There we would hold each other and gaze into each other's eyes, professing our love and commitment, and acknowledging the pain of letting go. Despite our tears, our hearts were full. During one of our last cuddle times, Marvin said, "When I look in your eyes, I see the young girl I married. You were the right choice."

Although Marvin recovered from his broken ribs, his nausea became more chronic in November. It made him suffer but little could be done to relieve it. Slipping out of his wheelchair in December caused a spinal compression. The three of us discussed when would be best to bring hospice back in to help medicate his nausea. Disengaging the heart pump meant his death would come sooner. We decided to get through Marvin's eighty-fourth birthday on December 16 and the holidays. In January, we removed the heart pump and called hospice.

Before hospice began, the three of us spent the weekend together laughing, crying and sharing whatever we needed to, because we knew once the medication protocol started, Marvin would lose consciousness. Aaron sang the songs he'd composed for his father one last time. Marvin returned to our bed for one last nap. Through my tears, I said, "I don't know what I'll do without you."

He answered, "You have passion for life. And now it is really your time to do for yourself. Paint, write, travel, make a life in Taos. No more caretaking!"

Hospice started January 13, 2021, with the medical management of his pain and nausea. Gradually, over the next few days his doses of morphine and lorazepam increased. On Saturday, January 16, Marvin told me my deceased father, Ed, smiled at him from the doorway.

What a relief to hear that my father, a touchstone in my life, had come to help my husband cross over. Marvin seemed pleased as well.

Although he was barely conscious, after this he would occasionally stir, mumbling, "I feel your warmth" and "I can count on you." Marvin had no food and only a little water for the eight days before he died. Despite being mentally ready, his body did not give in easily for his spirit to leave on its journey; his pulse remained strong and his kidneys functioned until the end.

For those ten days, Aaron and I kept vigil with Marvin. All of us slept together in our tiny den, Aaron on the loveseat and me on a mattress butting up to Marvin's hospital bed. Although Marvin was unresponsive, we took turns talking and singing to him, stroking him gently, reassuring him all was going according to plan. I even held his hand all night, with a rose quartz in between our palms, soaking in all the love vibrations. Rose quartz is reputed to be a crystal of universal and unconditional love. Later that stone was something I could hold onto that contained Marvin's energy. I will never forget how warm his hands were, until the very end, as he'd always complained they were cold. Someone told me this was his heart energy coming through.

Two days before he died, I was awakened at five am by Marvin's energy pulsating through me, communicating, "You are loved! Never doubt my love for you!" He was starting to transition. Then a dream followed. *"I was sitting on a bench, watching young people go into a small shop and come out wearing new outfits. Then a young man sat beside me and put his arm around me and told me 'not to worry; that new things were being tried out.'*

Aaron woke that morning to a kingfisher sitting outside our door. This bird had never been on our property before, nor has it been seen since. Kingfishers are considered to be sacred birds with control over the ocean waves. They "indicate a period of increased mental and spiritual activity" and "symbolize peace, promising prosperity and love."

Marvin's last breath came two days later. The transitioning process is different for everyone; it can be rapid or take days or weeks. Marvin's spirit departed at three pm on January 25, on a beautiful, sunny day. Aaron and I were in the kitchen. I was correcting his song project for Marvin. This was Marvin's forte. He was the grammatical and spelling expert in our family. He was fondly called "Chief Red Pen" at one of his executive director jobs over the years. Something told me to check on Marvin when I finished my corrections at three pm. His breaths were slower and more spread out. I called Aaron into the room and within minutes Marvin took his last breath. We later joked that Marvin wanted to make sure we were finished with those corrections before he died.

Moments after his passing, I experienced being in the vortex of divine energy with Marvin, seeing him smile, doing what I call his New York City giggle, his beautiful legs dancing, while beaming at Aaron and me, with his hands over each of our crown chakras transmitting love and light. Every cell within me was vibrating, cracking open. Marvin was now at peace, free from pain and suffering, enjoying the love and light of our Divine Creator.

Resolution of our karmic connection was now complete. Aaron survived birth and I survived a knife to the belly for him to be born. Marvin would be the first of our trio to die in this lifetime. He felt forgiven for any wrongdoing from his past life and a sense of worth to have contributed to both Aaron's and my life emotionally and financially. He'd taken care of us, emotionally and financially in this lifetime, rather than allow us to be sacrificed as he'd done in the previous incarnation.

When I would care for him, he would just look at me and say, "I never knew you could love me this much." He would say similar things to Aaron, who was devoted to his dad during those final months. To be able to help someone who so loved and appreciated us was a gift for both of us. It surprised me that I had given over to loving Marvin in every way. And, that I was allowing myself to be loved in return.

Our last love notes to each other:

Dearest Marvin…

You have given me much for which I am truly grateful.
You are steadfast and unwavering, true and dependable.
"A good man," my mother said.

You are someone I pushed against to discover more of myself.
You withstood my outbursts and changing moods even when I didn't understand them myself.

You helped me become more assertive and supported my dreams even when you were not part of them. I learned to embrace my feminine side as I watched you embrace yours.

There is beauty in being soft, gentle and receptive.

Together we endured a trail of pregnancy losses and birthed a beautiful, loving son. Our greatest accomplishment together, Aaron Taos. He shares our traits, good and bad, but he is definitely of us. I am truly grateful that you shared in raising Aaron, giving him qualities and experiences that I could not. You were patient and understanding of his night fears when he was a child, his rites of passage during adolescence, and his anxieties in becoming a young adult. I treasure the times of us three, traveling or being at home. We form the perfect triangle in our family.

I take pride in your professional accomplishments and your wisdom in financial matters. Many have benefited from your pioneering work in the gambling field and you being their therapist. You leave Aaron and me financial resources so our lives will continue comfortably after yours.

What I came to understand later in our lives together is your sensitivity and gentleness. I can see now that I hurt you at times with words or actions. I apologize for whatever I did or however I was trying to defend or assert myself. We had our share of times of tension and emotional separation as we each became who we needed to be.

I am glad that these last several years we found our love for each other greater than before with more laughs, conversations and time together. Traveling to our home in Truth or Consequences, NM, fishing on Elephant Butte Lake, spending time on Captiva Island or Port of the Islands, Florida, will always be treasured memories of our time together.

It would be a grand thing to bask in the Light and Love of each other forever. But that cannot be on this earth. Let us be thankful for what we have had together and for our wisdom to be together all these years.

I like to think that we three completed our karma in this lifetime. You, the high priest in another life, sacrificed our son and me to die young not knowing life or our togetherness as a family. In this life, you came through for Aaron and me, giving of yourself to become a family and provide us futures to live our dreams and aspirations. In return, you received our love and gratitude. All is forgiven. All ends in love and beauty. All is as it should be.

I will miss my partner, lover and friend.

There will be many days lived in sorrow after you leave.
But there will be many more days lived in celebration of our lives well lived.

We will meet again amongst the stars and ethers.

Travel well, Love. Be well, wherever your spirit takes Thee.

Your precious, Ruby (Catherine)

From Marvin:

HAPPY BIRTHDAY TO MY PRECIOUS RUBY SOULMATE FOREVER!!

May the next 10+ years be filled with creative energy in your painting, writing, Shamanic work and in ways yet to be discovered.

Be at peace in knowing that you have given me so much—loving me deeply with devotion to my wellbeing. I have unending gratitude that you have shared so much of your life and love with me.

Throughout this difficult time, our love shines brightly—and it's wonderful!

Loving you always!!
Your Marvin

(((

CHAPTER 24
Afterwards

What has it been like for me in the first year since Marvin's death? Challenging at times but with peaceful moments as well. During the first few months, February through April, I was mostly in rest and relief mode. After the weight of caregiving was lifted, my life was my own again for the first time since 2017. Aaron and I emptied three rooms full of boxed papers Marvin had brought home after retiring from his two executive director positions. While sorting those papers we found personal items, like Marvin's letters to his parents when he was in his twenties, teaching in Ethiopia and traveling around Europe. Reminiscent of my travels in South America in my twenties, these were more proof of our shared patterns.

Aaron took 80 boxes to the town dump. This made space for me to take over Marvin's office to write this book. The basement space has been repurposed too. Now I can hold shamanic painting classes there, which shows the benefit of making practical changes.

Aaron developed an excruciating, painful hip issue which made it hard for him to sit down comfortably. My caregiving skills were restarted for a couple of weeks until effective treatment was found. I was also dealing with settling Marvin's estate and drawing up new legal documents for myself. These were tedious tasks requiring time and money but necessary. It's amazing that dying requires such an expense and is taxed to boot!

Early on in the second three-month phase (May-July), the sadness I was feeling at the loss of Marvin turned into despair. There was a period of questioning the adage "to have loved and lost was better than to never have loved at all." I missed him so much! Such deep grief became a daily reality. A brief trip with Aaron to my house in Taos, New Mexico, and some energy work helped me through it. Then life became more difficult when I was forced to deal with major home crises back in Connecticut: our 45-year-old well collapsed and I was without water for six weeks; I was scammed for $1,300; and the septic backed up into the house because of a blockage in the main pipe (literally shit everywhere)! What was the universe telling me?? LET GO of the past and move on!

During this time, I also had to sell Marvin's boat…the only item that was not in both our names. I had to file papers with probate and make trips to the DMV for proper identification and ownership before I could sell it. When the boat was ready to sell, it was up to me, with no knowledge about the boat or how it worked, to make the sale. Aaron was in Europe for the summer so I had to rely on his friends and others to help me through the process. Luckily, used boats were in demand so it was sold quickly to a nice family who promised to take care of it and carry on our family's father-son fishing and boating traditions. I was sad to see the boat being trailered for the last time down our driveway. It was the vehicle for Marvin's pleasure; a vestige of Marvin.

Somehow during this time period, I picked up this memoir, which I had started in the '90s, and began writing again. There were days that I just wanted to sit and snack on the couch and escape to an exotic television series from Asia or Turkey. But I would hear Marvin's voice saying, "get up there and write." So I did most times. I thought writing this memoir was taking on too much too soon, but it actually turned into being an excellent tool for grieving. It helped me be present with loss and love as I recorded my experiences with Marvin.

In August, I traveled back out to Taos for five weeks, bringing along my good friend, Lianne, for the first two weeks. We had known each other since the early '90s, often sharing artistic pursuits and fun outings. Together we traveled to New York and New Mexico to study painting with artists there. In 2001 we had even gone to Italy for two weeks with our Italian-born teacher, Alex Shundi. Lianne became my Saturday night "date" for dinner and a movie after Marvin died. It was extremely important to have someone consistently in my life as I tried to move forward in my grief. Although we did not spend much time discussing Marvin, it was necessary to have someone to laugh with and discuss important worldly matters as I dealt with his absence. Unfortunately, I lost Lianne to cancer in April 2023. I am bereft but forever grateful for her presence in my life, especially those last two years.

Those weeks in Taos were so peaceful, sitting with the sunsets and allowing myself to just be with the land. I was finally able to settle in the house I'd bought two years prior. COVID and Marvin's failing health had prevented my doing it sooner. I began meeting people and feeling the stirrings of new energy. When it came time to return to Connecticut, I did not want to go. While in the Taos shuttle, making the two-and-a-half-hour trip to the Albuquerque airport, my tears were flowing. Thirty-two years prior I made the same drive when leaving Taos after my first summer there as a sculpture apprentice. Such a sad parting. I told myself the same thing I did then: *I will be back.*

Returning to Connecticut in mid-September was difficult and brought up another wave of grief, especially when no one was there to greet me, and the house was quiet and dark. But I had my work with clients, painting classes to facilitate, and the business of life to attend to, so I got "back in the saddle." Around October 22, there was a reemergence of deep grieving. It was also when the sun moved into the eighth sign of the zodiac, Scorpio, which is all about swimming in the deep end of emotion. Scorpio is the "rising sign" on my astrological birth chart. I was grieving for Marvin, but also for other family members I had lost. Hospice sent a letter saying that about nine months after a loved one dies, the "anniversary syndrome" kicks in with the anticipation of the anniversary date of death. It was normal for me to have unsettling feelings and emotions coming out of nowhere. They were right on.

As I approach this one year anniversary of Marvin's death, I am down in the depths of loss with him not being here. At times I feel his energy come to me when I ask for it and there is a presence I experience. However, I miss his warm embrace and words of wisdom especially when I start getting myself wound up about something. He was a calming, grounding energy for me. What I miss most is how his eyes would light up and twinkle when I would come into the room. He would often wake up early those last few months when he was mostly confined to his hospital bed and ask the caregiver, "Where is my bride…the beautiful woman I married?" Or he would call me his little mermaid, "merms" for short, when I went off to the pool for aquatic exercise.

I could not receive all the love he was giving me then as I was so preoccupied with his dying and giving him all that he needed in the process. My only regret was not soaking in all the love coming my way since I was preparing myself for loss and letting go. During meditative times now, I ask to receive his love and experience the heat and energy in doing so. In this way, I still feel connected to Marvin and continue to receive his love. Some have told me they are closer to their deceased loved ones in death than they were in life. Many have written and spoken about the veil between the living and dead being thin and accessible. Perhaps that is where we should direct our energy in relating to Spirit, rather than getting lost in regrets and the unfinished business of the living.

I want to underscore the cyclical nature of all things. All beginnings have endings and all endings have opportunities to start something new. Sometimes we do not know what is possible until we have truly lost someone or something. Possibilities cannot show themselves while we are focused elsewhere. It is in the fallow season or the in-between space of creation and destruction, in the darkness and uncertainty, that the seeds of hope and possibility arise. I feel the stirrings of new energy that will, in time, come into the Light and take form.

)))

CHAPTER 25
Newfound Wonder

Almost a year after my husband's death, on December 11, 2021, I had my first experience with plant medicine. This occurred during the first quarter phase of the moon, when exactly half the moon is illuminated and the other half dark. This chocolate ceremony consisted of drinking cacao mixed with psilocybin from mushrooms, which was often done in earlier Mesoamerican cultures when they consumed this "medicine." The Aztecs called the sacred mushrooms *teonanacatl,* meaning flesh of the gods, and cacao *theobroma cacao,* meaning food of the gods. This powerful combination increases the effects because the mushroom opens the mind, and the cacao opens the heart.[19]

Since I had never taken psilocybin before, I did not know what to expect. The experience was mostly pleasant, except for the typical nausea that accompanies it. Time slowed down; what seemed like hours were actually minutes. Each of the participants stated out loud what their intentions were for this experience as we drank "the medicine." Mine was a request for information to guide me in the next phase of my life. In the first few moments after ingesting it, the medicine told me "I am in service to you"! Then I saw my heart above me and was told, "Your big, beautiful heart that has fed many, now feeds you." Many beautiful, vibrant colors appeared in endless patterns and shapes with the message to discover and record these images in paint. Then a heartfelt communication came through from my paternal grandmother, Alice, and my mother, Arline.

Both of them had lived lives of service to others and not to self. Yet they were teaching me about self-love and joy; the love and joy that I need for myself, not just for others around me. It was the Divine Feminine speaking through them, reminding me to receive love from others, and myself, and to own the fullness of who I am, living in my Light. The entire experience left me feeling deeply satisfied, as though I have completed this phase of my life with its theme of deep loss. Now I am ready to move on, to follow the threads that were revealed and to continue weaving these strands of my life.

One delightful revelation has been the growing, deeply loving relationship with my son. Over the years, ours has been a close relationship, although it was triangular, to include Marvin. Since I understood it was most likely that I'd outlive his father, I'd always encouraged the two of them to spend father-son time together. I presumed there would be more opportunities to be with my son later on. This has indeed happened. Developing such a close relationship with my adult son has been a pleasant surprise. In my family of origin this was not the case. After college, I'd gone out on my own, to seek close relationships with friends rather than family. I loved my parents and kept in contact, but I shared my life experiences and confidences with friends.

Now, Aaron wants to spend time with me. We share life's triumphs and concerns, even becoming good travel companions on recent trips to Scandinavia and Turkey. We did a fun road trip from Taos to Los Angeles this past year. And Aaron has also provided valuable feedback on the contents of this book, as well as suggestions about other aspects of my life. Ours is a two-way relationship, with meaningful giving and receiving.

This was not always the case when Aaron was younger. During his early adolescence we were estranged for a time. Most parents experience this individuation phase as their children detach and differentiate themselves. While separation is necessary and healthy, it can be painful and heartbreaking for parents when their children become self-absorbed and uncaring. I experienced this with my son and we're both grateful to see our family has managed to navigate this difficult transition. I remember helpful advice from friends, whose children were already grown adults, "Not to worry, Aaron will turn around in his 20s. You will have a loving relationship again with your son." And they were right. When my son was about to graduate from Vassar College in 2013, I received the most beautiful, heartfelt, appreciative letter from Aaron on Mother's Day. Since then our relationship has continued to improve, more so now that Marvin is gone. My hope is we continue to stay as close even when Aaron has his own family in the future.

Writing this memoir has been therapeutic, not just to grieve the death of my life partner, but for reevaluating my life via this intensely thorough reflection. Through the process of writing I have revisited many experiences in my past. This makes me realize I need to surrender what has gone on before. *Surrender.* I have always despised the word, but it holds true for where I currently am in my life. I need to weep, and weep, and weep some more — letting go of what was, knowing it will remain part of me. Working on this book has helped me process and integrate so much that happened in my life this time around…to bring it in and to let it go. In some ways the lessons have waxed and waned just like the moon.

POSTSCRIPT
January 8, 2024

Today I woke up feeling out of sorts, my body uncoordinated and my mind unclear. Several times I broke down in tears. *What is happening to me? Am I getting sick?* I pushed myself along however since I had my yearly dental appointment at 1:30 pm. I remembered that when I am not focused upon anything else, except to get myself somewhere, I'm in a state of being when divine intervention can more easily seep in and give me clarity. As I left the house, I heard the word *Beware.*

Surprisingly, there was no traffic on the section I had to travel on — Interstate 95 in Connecticut — so my drive was easy. The warning to *Beware* must refer to something else so I kept paying attention. When the dental hygienist came to collect me from the waiting area, she called me "Ruby."

This was a surprise! For years I've seen the same hygienist. She normally calls me Catherine, my given name. She also wondered why she used Ruby instead, my spirit name.

Some of the explanation was in the case notes she'd just reviewed prior to my appointment. Ten-year-old-notes from 2014 had "Ruby" at the top of the page. The hygienist apologized, saying she was not sure why she had said Ruby when she has always called me Catherine. I assured her calling me Ruby was fine, but I was puzzled about why the dental office had Ruby written in their notes. The appointment went on as usual except that our connection felt more personal during this visit.

Being called Ruby is a reminder of all that name means, and the path I am on, as described in Chapter Thirteen. Marvin also called me Ruby more often than not. Maybe this was why I needed to *Beware* today, so as not to miss the prompting to be true to my Ruby identity and pay attention to my "heart-truth." Or as the Ravens told me in Chapter One, "You are here this time around to learn the workings of the heart." I continued to reflect upon this divine message that day.

After the dental appointment, I returned to my car. No car was parked next to mine on the driver's side. Instead there was a large paper sign on the ground with the numbers "717" on it. I thought this was odd, but when I looked up the numerical association later at home this is what it said:

"Angel number 717 means you're on the right path toward spiritual enlightenment. It's a reminder to trust your intuition as you approach a new phase of your life. 717 can also mean you're on the verge of a new romance or a deeper relationship, a reunion with your twin flame, or even the next step of your career."

This was a message of encouragement and affirmation. Yet I broke down in tears once again, missing my husband… I *wanted him to be here with me at this time in my life supporting new chapters in my life, not someone else.* Engulfed by grief, I had to lie down to console myself. I'd suspected this month of January would be rough since it was the anniversary month of Marvin's death, three years ago. But this amount of weeping seemed absurd. I gave into it and rested.

Then a text came from a friend who sent a photo taken two weeks earlier on her visit to my home. We were up in my studio, arms around each other. This friend always impressed me with her ability to laugh and have fun, even after the profound loss of her forty-year-old daughter. *How can one suffer such a tragedy, feel the depths of sadness, yet be so full of life?* Her example was heartening rather than disheartening. *Be aware of this lesson.* Yet my mind thinks it knows the heart holds all; for without deep sadness, there would be no deep joy. These extremes increase our capacities for learning, loving and understanding our lives as a whole.

Being reminded of the heart connection proves its importance. With this came an epiphany, just two days after the Catholic holy day of the Epiphany had passed, as if to further prompt me to put all these pieces together. *Don't miss what all this means.* Remembering the dental office incident earlier that day inspired me to get out of bed and get on my computer. I realized the final chapter of this book needs to explicitly address these "workings of the heart."

For me this means learning to follow my heart-truth. This includes cultivating an awareness of all the intuitive nudges, which may only hold meanings for us: our form of symbolic language and our method of piecing together what our minds might miss. To know what is truly inspired by love not just mental logic. The heart's wisdom is greater than the mind's, but our hearts must work with our minds to express coherently, via word and deed, what love knows to be true. To act from love, not fear, not loss, not pain. Fear is defensive. It distances us from ourselves and each other. It obscures the truth. In trying to protect us, fear will misguide us. When I have followed my "heart-truth," the path of Rubybear, I am most often pleased with the results and can feel the fullness of my being expanding to include my soul's potential.

This memoir is now complete…further validated by a dream and a vision that occurred three days after the dental visit. In the dream I was pregnant, about to give birth. Happily holding the hand of a man (presumably my husband, Marvin), who was supporting me through this new type of birthing process. My left hand was held in his right, receiving his energy. In the vision, my guides were showing me my book, wrapped and tied with a bow, a gift ready to be given to the world.

Getting to know ourselves, to discover our paths and to somehow find the affirmations and permissions to follow our hearts' truth can take a long time, as my story has shown. We need to support each other on these journeys, especially when it comes to the crucial decisions to follow the heart-truth paths of our souls. To be given the blessings of permission and assurance, as my departed mother and grandmother gave me during my cacao and mushroom ceremony, demonstrates why we must continue to pass along our heart-truths to others. As my journey continues, I look forward to working with others, supporting their awareness of who they are, what path they want to walk, and providing permission to become who they are. May we all grow into the Light of who we truly are!

To close, here is one more story of how spirit energies can support us when our hearts are troubled. Whenever I feel anxious these days, about being the only one left in the nest, I remember what I did when I felt the same kind of anxiety, the evening before Aaron departed for his college semester abroad in Madrid, Spain in 2012. To face my fears, I went on a shamanic journey.

I met up with Bear at the usual place where I begin my journeys. This involved jumping in our pond, swimming to the far side and going under water to the partially submerged "bear cave" of my imagination. Bear and I did our usual "pat down" greeting and then he took me to a clearing. There was my son and over his head was a huge crystal similar to one I owned. Through this crystal came refracted light in the four directions. It was magnificent! Many ancestors and spirit guides were walking through the streams of light. My son seemed to be in a different realm. I was awestruck and gaping at the scene.

After a few moments, Bear put his arm around me and praised me for my job in raising Aaron and told me it was time to move on. I was reluctant to leave but Bear firmly took me away down the path. I hung my head, feeling sad and lost, wondering what would become of me. Bear laughed and pointed down the path I was walking. In the distance, there was a shimmering, crystal palace. Bear told me that there was much more ahead and I had only to go explore the different rooms and find the treasures that awaited me there. I then felt my body regain its full size, and I became curious, infused with a sense of adventure instead of sadness. As I thanked Bear for these messages, there was an image of vertical arcs of light, going through my son, my husband and myself, connecting us far above and far below. And so it is!

And so may it be in an appropriate way for you too, dear readers.

FOR THOSE WHO HAVE FAR TO TRAVEL
AN EPIPHANY BLESSING

If you could see
the journey whole,
you might never
undertake it,
might never dare
the first step
that propels you
from the place
you have known
toward the place
you know not.

Call it
one of the mercies
of the road:
that we see it
only by stages
as it opens
before us,
as it comes into
our keeping,
step by
single step.

There is nothing
for it
but to go,
and by our going
take the vows
the pilgrim takes:

to be faithful to
the next step;
to rely on more
than the map;
to heed the signposts
of intuition and dream;
to follow the star that only you
will recognize;

to keep an open eye
for the wonders that
attend the path;
to press on
beyond distractions,
beyond fatigue,
beyond what would
tempt you
from the way.

There are vows
that only you
will know:
the secret promises
for your particular path
and the new ones
you will need to make
when the road
is revealed
by turns
you could not
have foreseen.

Keep them, break them,
make them again;
each promise becomes
part of the path,
each choice creates
the road
that will take you
to the place
where at last
you will kneel

to offer the gift
most needed—
the gift that only you
can give—
before turning to go
home by
another way.

– Jan Richardson

ACKNOWLEDGMENTS

The inspiration for writing this memoir came from living life with my husband, Marvin, and our son, Aaron Taos. Without either of them, these stories would not exist nor would my heart have been cracked open in the ways that it was. My gratitude to each of them continues to grow, even though Marvin is now in another dimension. I feel his supportive and loving presence, especially in the writing of this book and bringing it to completion. With Aaron, I am grateful that he continues to want me in his life in a meaningful way. We share a bond that grows stronger as we each walk a creative and adventurous path in our respective ways.

Much love and appreciation goes to my editor, Cynthia F. Davidson. Without your tremendous enthusiasm for the subject matter of my memoir and your brilliant insights, this book might not have reached its final stage. You held "my feet to the fire," to dig deeper into the essence of what I was writing about so the readers would understand and take away the importance of what I was trying to convey. Sometimes I resisted, but

I usually came around to your valuable input. You are without exception, a bright light upon this earth! Our editorial relationship was much like the waxing and waning of the moon; work on the book would be intense and then stop, sometimes for six months at a time, because life would get in the way. Perhaps that is a woman's way of being in the world; circling... attending to all that is needed of her...then coming back around again. But we both saw it through to the end since we knew the universe wanted it out there at this point in the earth's evolution.

Much gratitude goes to Betsy Lawyer Allinson who offered to fine-tune my manuscript making it the best version of itself. And many thanks to Jen Payne for designing this beautiful book, and to my early readers Aaron Taos, Wendy, Winter, Betsy, Gray and Lauren. Your invaluable support and comments were helpful in finalizing this manuscript.

Deep appreciation to all my clients over the years, and to the participants in my retreats and workshops for being present and courageous to grow more fully into who they are. I am honored that you chose me to be your guide through the challenging times in your lives.

And last, but not least, much love and thanks go to my "sister" guides, friends and family: Adele, Alex, Alice, Ann, Arline, Barb, Barbara, Betsey, Char, Chelan, Chris, Doris, Dorothy, Ed, Ellen, Elizabeth, Gwen, Jackie, Jan, Janis, Jeanie, Jeffrey, Joel, Karen, Kimberley, Kit, Leslie, Lianne, Linda, Luckey, Marilyn, Matthew, Melissa, Michael, Michelle, Nancy, Pam, Pat, Ramsey, Sandra, Sue, Susan, Susie, Sisters of the Drum, Synthia, Teina, Wendy, Winter, and the Women's Well (Interface 1995-6).

ENDNOTES

1   Solly, Meilan. "Cacao Was First Cultivated in South America, Not Mexico and Central America." October 30, 2018. (Source: www.smithsonianmag.com)

2   "The Royal History of Chocolate-An Expensive Taste." April 24, 2022. (Source: www.keylink.org/resources/The-Blog)

3   "Cacao Mama." 2014-2024. (Source: www.cacaomama.com)

4   Vidal, John. "Bolivia enshrines natural world's rights with equal status for Mother Earth." April 10, 2011. (Source: www.theguardian.com)

5   "Marvin A. Steinberg." January 29, 2021. (Source: www.legacy.com)

6   Moss, Robert. *Sidewalk Oracles: Playing with Signs, Symbols, and Synchronicity in Everyday Life.* Novato, CA: New World Library, 2015.

7   "The Mayan Pantheon: Gods and Goddesses." (Source: www.Historyonthenet.com)

8   Ardren, Traci. *Social Identities in the Classic Maya Northern Lowlands: Gender, Age, Memory and Place.* University of Texas Press: Austin, 2015.

9   Scherer, Andrew. *Mortuary Landscapes of the Classic Mayans: Rituals of Body and Soul.* University of Texas Press: Austin, 2015.

10 Rankin, Lissa., M.D. *Sacred Medicine: A Doctor's Quest to Unravel the Mysteries of Healing.* Louisville, CO: Sounds True, 2022.

11 Bensinger, Charles. *Chaco Canyon: Remembrance and Awakening.* Santa Fe, NM: Timewindow Publications, 1988.

12 Spiller, Jan, and McCoy, Karen. *Spiritual Astrology: A Path to Divine Awakening.* New York City, NY: Atria Books, 1988.

13 "Pregnancy loss leads to post-traumatic stress in one in three women." February 9, 2021. (Source: https://evidence.nihr.ac.uk)

14 McGuinnes, Devan. "Lost Pregnancies and Lost Loves: How Miscarriage Impacts Your Relationship." September 30, 2022. (Source: www.healthline.com)

15 Sams, Jamie, and Carson, David. *Medicine Cards: The Discovery of Power Through the Ways of Animals*. Santa Fe, NM: Bear & Company, Har/Crds edition,1992.

16 Forest, Ohky Simine. *Dreaming The Council Ways: True Native Teachings from the Red Lodge*. Newburyport, MA: RedWheel/Weiser, 2009.

17 Abram, David. *The Spell of the Sensuous*. New York City, NY: Vintage Books, 1997.

18 Source: www.sandraingerman.com

19 "Microdosing Psilocybin With Cacao: An Ancient Combination In A New Light". 2024. (Source: www.purekakaw.com)

BIBLIOGRAPHY

With appreciation for the authors who have influenced my life and work.

Abram, David. *The Spell of the Sensuous*. New York City, NY: Vintage Books, 1997.

Anderson, Sherry Ruth, and Hopkins, Patricia. *THE FEMININE FACE OF GOD: The Unfolding of the Sacred in Women*. New York City, NY: Bantam Books, 1991.

Andrews, Ted. *ANIMAL SPEAK: The Spiritual & Magical Powers of Creatures Great & Small*. St. Paul, MN: Llewellyn Publications, 2003.

Armstrong, Jim, and Armstrong, Anne. *Awakening the Divine Within Kundalini—The Gateway to Freedom*. Bloomington, IN: iUniverse, 2011.

Arrien, Angeles. *THE FOUR-FOLD WAY: Walking the Paths of the Warrior, Teacher, Healer and Visionary*. New York City, NY: HarperCollins, 1993.

Bensinger, Charles. *Chaco Canyon: Remembrance and Awakening*. Santa Fe, NM: Timewindow Publications, 1988.

Fisher, Joe. *THE CASE FOR REINCARNATION*. New York City, NY: Bantam Books, 1985.

Forest, Ohky Simine. *Dreaming The Council Ways: True Native Teachings from the Red Lodge*. Newburyport, MA: Red Wheel/Weiser, 2009.

Gibran, Kahil. *The Prophet*. New York City, NY: Knopf Publishing, 1923.

Gilligan, Carol. *IN A DIFFERENT VOICE: Psychological Theory and Women's Development*. Cambridge, MA: Harvard University Press, 1982.

Goldberg, Philip. *THE INTUITIVE EDGE: Understanding and Developing Intuition.* Los Angeles, CA: Jeremy P. Tarcher, 1983.

Hall, James A., M.D. *Jungian Dream Interpretation, A Handbook of Theory and Practice.* Toronto, Canada: Inner City Books, 1983.

Harkin, Chelan. *Susceptible to Light.* WA: Soulfruit Publishing, 2020.

Hart, Mickey. *DRUMMING AT THE EDGE OF MAGIC: A Journey into the Spirit of Percussion.* New York City, NY: HarperCollins, 1990.

Ingerman, Sandra. *Soul Retrieval: Mending the Fragmented Self.* San Francisco, CA: Harper One, 1991.

Ingerman, Sandra. *Medicine For The Earth: How To Transform Personal And Environmental Toxins.* New York City, NY: Harmony, 2001.

Ingerman, Sandra. *Shamanic Journeying: A Beginner's Guide.* Louisville, CO: Sounds True, 2004.

Ingerman, Sandra. *How to Heal Toxic Thoughts: Simple Tools For Personal Transformation.* New York City, NY: Sterling Ethos, 2007.

Ingerman, Sandra, and Wesselman, Hank. *Awakening To The Spirit World: The Shamanic Path of Direct Revelation.* Louisville, CO: Sounds True, 2010.

Ingerman, Sandra. *Walking In Light: The Everyday Empowerment of a Shamanic Life.* Louisville, CO: Sounds True, 2014.

Ingerman, Sandra, and Roberts, Llyn. *Walking Through Darkness: A Nature-Based Path to Navigating Suffering and Loss.* New York City, NY: Sterling Ethos, 2023.

Jung, C. G. *Aspects of the Feminine, Bollingen Series.* Princeton, NJ: Princeton University Press, 1992.

Krippner, Stanley. *Perchance to Dream: The Frontiers of Dream Psychology.* Hauppauge, NY: Nova Science Publishers, 2009.

Lipton, Bruce. *The Biology of Belief: Unleashing the Power of Consciousness, Matter, & Miracles.* Santa Rosa, CA: Mountain of Love/Elite Books, 2005.

Miller, Jean Baker, M.D. *Toward a New Psychology of Women.* Boston, MA: Beacon Press, 1986.

Moss, Robert. *DREAMING THE SOUL BACK HOME: Shamanic Dreaming for Healing and Becoming Whole.* Novato, CA: New World Library, 2012.

Moss, Robert. *Sidewalk Oracles: Playing with Signs, Symbols, and Synchronicity in Everyday Life.* Novato, CA: New World Library, 2015.

Murdock, Maureen. *The Heroine's Journey: Women's Quest for Wholeness.* Boston, MA: Shambhala, 1990.

Myss, Caroline. *Sacred Contracts: Awakening Your Divine Potential.* New York City, NY: Three Rivers Press, 2003.

Netherton, Morris, and Shiffrin, Nancy. *Past Lives Therapy.* New York City, NY: Morrow, 1978.

Netherton, Morris, and Paul, Thomas. *Past Life Therapy: Past Life Regression Special Edition with Past Life Therapy Center.* CA: Dr. Morris Netherton, 2013.

Netherton, Morris. *The Netherton Method of Past Life Awareness and Integration: A Modality for Success.* Scotts Valley, CA: CreateSpace Independent Publishing Platform, 2015.

Netherton, Morris. *Strangers in the Land of Confusion.* Scotts Valley, CA: CreateSpace Independent Publishing Platform, 2015.

Noble, Viki. *MOTHERPEACE: A Way to the Goddess through Myth, Art, and Tarot.* San Francisco, CA: Harper, 1994.

Page, Christine R. M.D. *THE HEART OF THE GREAT MOTHER: Spiritual Initiation, Creativity, and Rebirth.* Rochester, VT: Inner Traditions, 2020.

Plotkin, Bill. *SOULCRAFT: Crossing into the Mysteries of Nature and Psyche.* Novato, CA: New World Library, 2003.

Rankin, Lissa., M.D. *Sacred Medicine: A Doctor's Quest to Unravel the Mysteries of Healing.* Louisville, CO: Sounds True, 2022.

Redmond, Layne. *WHEN THE DRUMMERS WERE WOMEN: A Spiritual History of Rhythm.* New York City, NY: Three Rivers Press, 1997.

Richardson, Jan. *Circle of Grace: A Book of Blessings for the Seasons.* Orlando, FL: Wanton Gospeller Press, 2015.

Rodegast, Pat, and Stanton, Judith. *Emmanuel's Book III: What Is an Angel Doing Here?* New York City, NY: Bantam, 1994.

Sams, Jamie, and Carson, David. *Medicine Cards: The Discovery of Power Through the Ways of Animals.* Santa Fe, NM: Bear & Company, Har/Crds edition,1992.

Spiller, Jan, and McCoy, Karen. *Spiritual Astrology: A Path to Divine Awakening.* New York City, NY: Atria Books, 1988.

Wambach, Helen. *RELIVING PAST LIVES: The Evidence Under Hypnosis.* New York City, NY: Harper & Row, 1978.

Welwood, John, ED. *AWAKENING THE HEART: East/West Approaches to Psychotherapy and the Healing Relationship.* Boulder, CO: Shambhala, 1983.

QUESTIONS FOR DISCUSSION

1. What were the main themes of this book? How did the author bring those themes to life?

2. How do you feel about the book? Which emotions did it evoke?

3. What aspects of the story could you most relate to? Least?

4. Did you find this book satisfying to read? Why or why not?

5. What did you learn from this book? Were you surprised by anything in particular?

6. Has chocolate played any special role in your life?

7. What sort of relationship do you have with the moon and its phases?

8. Have you experienced pregnancy loss and/or infertility issues? If you are walking the motherhood path, what have been your key challenges?

9. Have you endured a major loss? How has this changed you? In what ways have you dealt with the challenges of significant loss(es) in your life? Did this book provide any insights, approaches or tools you can use to better cope with any losses, current or future ones?

10. How have dreams, synchronicities and meaningful coincidences influenced your life?

11. Do you rely upon your intuition? Often or only occasionally? Were there times you wished you had followed your intuition and did not? What happened when you ignored it? And were there times you wished you hadn't used your intuition?

12. Are you familiar with shamanism? What aspects of shamanism do you already practice in your life? What aspects would you like to add?

13. Do you have relationships with people who give you the feeling that your connection with them extends beyond this lifetime? How do you sense this? What have you done about it? Share examples about the ways you've used to discern these connections.

Aaron, Ruby & Marvin in Connecticut, 2017

Ruby in Taos, New Mexico, 2023

CATHERINE NOGAS STEINBERG, LMFT

earned a B.A. degree from Mount Holyoke College and
an M.A. degree from the University of Connecticut.
She has over forty years of psychotherapy experience with
individuals, couples, families and groups in Guilford,
Connecticut. Catherine is also a shamanic practitioner, artist,
and workshop/retreat facilitator in Connecticut and New Mexico.
A central theme in her work is empowering women to become
who they truly want to be. Catherine, a.k.a Rubybear, is nourished
by adventure and travel to sacred sites and natural places of
beauty. Visit www.catherinensteinberg.com for more information.

www.ingramcontent.com/pod-product-compliance
Lightning Source LLC
Chambersburg PA
CBHW050442150626
46551CB00028B/1101